D1329999

Ancient Aramaic and Hebrew Letters

Society of Biblical Literature

Writings from the Ancient World

Theodore J. Lewis, General Editor

Associate Editors

Billie Jean Collins
Jerrold S. Cooper
Edward L. Greenstein
Jo Ann Hackett
Richard Jasnow
Ronald J. Leprohon
C. L. Seow
Niek Veldhuis

Number 14
Ancient Aramaic and Hebrew Letters
by James M. Lindenberger
Edited by Kent Harold Richards

ANCIENT ARAMAIC AND

HEBREW LETTERS

Second Edition

by
James M. Lindenberger

Edited by
Kent Harold Richards

Society of Biblical Literature
Atlanta

Library of Congress Cataloging-in-Publication Data

Lindenberger, James M.
    Ancient Aramaic and Hebrew letters / [prepared and translated] by James M. Lindenberger ; Edited by Kent H. Richards. — Rev. ed.
        p. cm. — (Writings from the ancient world ; no. 14)
        Includes bibliographical references and index.
    ISBN 1-58983-036-9
    1. Aramaic letters. 2. Aramaic letters—Translations into English. 3. Hebrew letters. 4. Hebrew letters—Translations into English. 5. Middle East—History—To 622—Sources. I. Lindenberger, James M. II. Richards, Kent Harold, 1939– III. Title. IV. Series.
    PJ5208.A2 L55 2003b
    492'.29—dc21   2002154284

11 10 09 08 07 06 05 04 03   5 4 3 2 1

Printed in the United States of America
on acid-free paper

Contents

Series Editor's Foreword

Writings from the Ancient World is designed to provide up-to-date, readable English translations of writings recovered from the ancient Near East.

The series is intended to serve the interests of general readers, students, and educators who wish to explore the ancient Near Eastern roots of Western civilization or to compare these earliest written expressions of human thought and activity with writings from other parts of the world. It should also be useful to scholars in the humanities or social sciences who need clear, reliable translations of ancient Near Eastern materials for comparative purposes. Specialists in particular areas of the ancient Near East who need access to texts in the scripts and languages of other areas will also find these translations helpful. Given the wide range of materials translated in the series, different volumes will appeal to different interests. However, these translations make available to all readers of English the world's earliest traditions as well as valuable sources of information on daily life, history, religion, and the like in the preclassical world.

The translators of the various volumes in this series are specialists in the particular languages and have based their work on the original sources and the most recent research. In their translations they attempt to convey as much as possible of the original texts in fluent, current English. In the introductions, notes, glossaries, maps, and chronological tables, they aim to provide the essential information for an appreciation of these ancient documents.

Covering the period from the invention of writing (by 3000 B.C.E.) down to the conquests of Alexander the Great (ca. 330 B.C.E.), the ancient Near East comprised northeast Africa and southwest Asia. The cultures represented within these limits include especially Egyptian, Sumerian, Babylonian, Assyrian, Hittite, Ugaritic, Aramean, Phoenician, and Israelite. It is hoped that Writings from the Ancient World will eventually produce translations of most of the many different genres attested in these cultures: letters (official and private), myths, diplomatic documents, hymns, law collections, monumental inscriptions, tales, and administrative records, to mention but a few.

Significant funding was made available by the Society of Biblical Literature for the preparation of this volume. In addition, those involved in preparing this volume have received financial and clerical assistance from their respective institutions. Were it not for these expressions of confidence in our work, the arduous tasks of preparation, translation, editing, and publication could not have been accomplished or even undertaken. It is the hope of all who have worked on these texts or supported this work that Writings from the Ancient World will open up new horizons and deepen the humanity of all who read these volumes.

Theodore J. Lewis
Johns Hopkins University

Abbreviations

AAB	*An Aramaic Bibliography,* vol. 1 (Fitzmyer and Kaufman 1992)
AD	*Aramaic Documents of the Fifth Century B.C.* (Driver 1954, 1965)
AIBL	Académie des Inscriptions et Belles-Lettres, Paris
AP	*Aramaic Papyri of the Fifth Century B.C.* (Cowley 1923)
Arch. Mus.	Archaeological Museum, Cairo University
ASAE	*Annales du Service des antiquités de l'Egypte*
BA	*Biblical Archaeologist*
BAR	*Biblical Archaeology Review*
BASOR	*Bulletin of the American Schools of Oriental Research*
BM	British Museum, London
BMAP	*The Brooklyn Museum Aramaic Papyri* (Kraeling 1953)
BZAW	Beihefte zur Zeitschrift für die alttestamentliche Wissenschaft
CAL	*Comprehensive Aramaic Lexicon* (see Kaufman, Fitzmyer, and Sokoloff 2001)
CIS	*Corpus inscriptionum semiticarum* (AIBL 1889)
Clermont-Ganneau	Clermont-Ganneau Collection, AIBL, Paris
DAE	*Documents araméens d'Egypte* (Grelot 1972)
DJD	Discoveries in the Judaean Desert
Eg. Mus.	Egyptian Museum, Cairo
HAHL	*Handbook of Ancient Hebrew Letters* (Pardee 1982)
IEJ	*Israel Exploration Journal*

IM	Israel Museum, Jerusalem
JAOS	*Journal of the American Oriental Society*
JBL	*Journal of Biblical Literature*
JNES	*Journal of Near Eastern Studies*
JUM	Jordan University Museum, Amman
KAI	*Kanaanäische und aramäische Inschriften* (Donner and Röllig 1966–69)
Lib.	library
O.	ostracon
P.	papyrus
PN	personal name
RES	*Répertoire d'épigraphie sémitique* (AIBL 1900–1968)
SBLWAW	Society of Biblical Literature Writings from the Ancient World
St. Mus.	Staatliche Museen, Berlin
TADA	*Textbook of Aramaic Documents from Ancient Egypt*, 1 (Porten and Yardeni 1986)
TADD	*Textbook of Aramaic Documents from Ancient Egypt*, 4 (Porten and Yardeni 1999)
VA	Vorderasiatische Abteilung

Scribal Abbreviations in Original Texts

′א	ארדב, ארדבן	*ardab*(s)
′ב	בת	*bath*(s)
לף	אלף	(one) thousand
′מ	מנה	*mina*(s)
′ש	שקל, שקלם, תקל, תקלן	shekel(s)
√	*letek* (one-half *homer*)	
Ͱ	*homer*	

Explanation of Signs

[...]	Gap in the text. The approximate length of the gap is indicated in the original texts, but not in the translation.
שלם]	Single brackets enclose restorations.
שׁ	Damaged letter, the identification of which is reasonably certain.
[שׁ]	Visible traces suitable to the restored letter, but not necessarily requiring it.
[̊]	Trace of an unidentifiable letter.
כי . זכר	Dot indicates a word-divider in the original.
< >	Modern editorial addition.
{ }	Modern editorial deletion.
{{ }}	Erasure by the ancient scribe.
ˆשלםˆ	Supralinear addition by the ancient scribe.
/	Editorial separation of two words written without an intervening space.
[At sunset]	Italics indicate translation of words conjecturally restored, or the assumed sense where no original can be restored. Also used for editorial comment, e.g., [several names are lost].
'שׁ, etc.	Indicates a single letter used by the ancient scribe as an abbreviation. See list of abbreviations.

Chronological Table

IMPERIAL POWERS	JUDAH	DATES	TEXT NOS.	EVENTS
ASSYRIA				
Esarhaddon (680–669)				
Ashurbanipal (668–627)	Josiah (640–609)			
Sin-shar-ishkun (?–612)		650	1	
Ashur-uballit II (611–609)	Jehoahaz (609)		50, 50a, 50b	612–609 fall of Assyria
BABYLONIA			52?	
Nabopolassar (625–605)	Jehoiakim (609–598)		2	
Nebuchadnezzar II (604–562)	Jehoiachin (598/597)	600	51–67	597 Judah surrenders first deportation
Amel-Marduk (561–560)	Zedekiah (597–587)		68	587 fall of Jerusalem
Neriglissar (559–556)			69	
Labashi-Marduk (556)				Babylonian exile
Nabonidus (555–539)		550		

PERSIA	JUDAH (governors)	EGYPT (satraps)	DATES	TEXT NOS.	PALESTINE AND EGYPT	GREECE AND ASIA MINOR
Cyrus (550–530)	Shesh-bazzar (ca. 538)				540 Babylon falls to Cyrus 539 return of Judean exiles	
Cambyses (529–522)		Aryandes			525 Cambyses conquers Egypt 520–515 Jerusalem temple rebuilt	
Darius I (521–486)	Zerubbabel (515) Elnathan (late 6th)	Farnadata (–486?)	500	3–11a 70	486–483 Egypt rebels	499 rebellion of Ionian cities 490 Persian defeat at Marathon
Xerxes I (485–465)	Ahazi (early 5th)	Achaemenes (481?–459)				480 Persia invades Greece, defeated at Salamis
Artaxerxes I (464–424)	Ezra? Nehemiah (445–?)	Arshama (454–403?)	450	12–29	465–454 Egypt rebels (Inaros) Sin-uballit (Sanballat) governor of Samaria	459–456 Herodotus visits Egypt 448 rebellion of Megabyzus in Asia Minor
Xerxes II (424)	Bagavahya			11	410–407 Arshama on leave in Persia 410 Elephantine temple destroyed	431–404 Peloponnesian Wars
Darius II (423–405)				30–36		
Artaxerxes II (404–359)			400	37–49	404 Egypt rebels (Amyrtaeus) 399 accession of Nepherites	

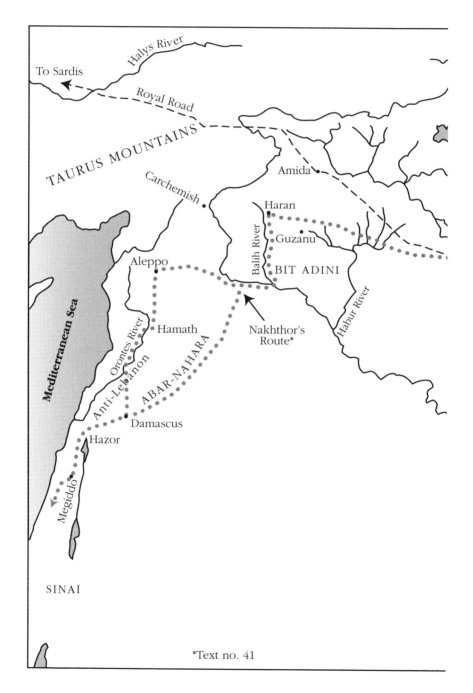

*Text no. 41

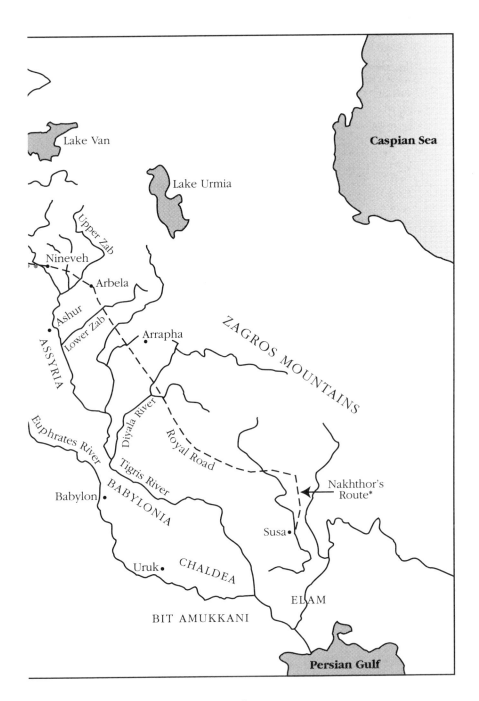

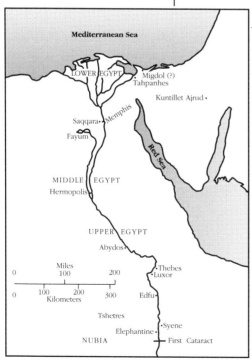

Acknowledgments

I would like to acknowledge the generous financial support of the National Endowment for the Humanities at the initial stages of research and the support of the H. R. MacMillan Fund of the Vancouver School of Theology throughout the project, especially in providing funding for a sabbatical leave at Duke Divinity School during which the revisions were completed. The library staff of the Vancouver School of Theology and Duke Divinity School libraries were unstinting in their help on bibliographic matters. Special thanks are due to Kent H. Richards for the skill and tact he has brought to his task as editor of both the original edition and the revision. Two skilled research assistants, Frances Dearman and Janice A. Guthrie, did much to facilitate the task of revision, as well as offering valuable suggestions on style and content. I am grateful to Bob Buller for his meticulous copy editing of the manuscript, without which many inconsistencies and inaccuracies would have slipped through. The maps are the collaborative work of Patti Zazulak and Bob Buller. And a final word of gratitude to Susan Smyth Lindenberger, who has read the manuscript repeatedly as it progressed and has provided support in a variety of other ways too numerous to mention.

This book is dedicated to the memory of my parents, John Blackwell Lindenberger and Virginia Gray Lindenberger.

Introduction

I. Overview

THE FIRST EDITION OF *Ancient Aramaic and Hebrew Letters* was published in 1994, fourth in the series Writings from the Ancient World. The original intent of the volume was to offer a readable anthology containing the better-preserved letters extant in Aramaic and Hebrew (excluding those found in the Hebrew Bible) down to the time of Alexander the Great. In addition, a tiny group of letters in Edomite, Ammonite, and Phoenician, one in each language, was included.

In keeping with that intent, the new edition includes nine new texts. Some of these have been published only since 1994 (nos. 50a, 50b, 70, 71); several fragments were already known but had not at that time been recognized as containing epistolary formulas (67a); a few others were added that should perhaps have been included in the first edition (11a, 25a, 27b, 67b).

Not only are more texts now known, but substantial new contributions have been added to the relevant secondary literature. There are new editions of some of the texts themselves, in particular Porten and Yardeni (1999) on the Aramaic ostraca, and Renz (1995) on the Hebrew letters. Significant new studies on the grammar have appeared: Muraoka and Porten (1998) on the Aramaic texts from Egypt, and Gogel (1998) on the Hebrew texts. A major new lexicon covering all of the material has been published (Hoftijzer and Jongeling 1995), as has a new study on Northwest Semitic epistolography (Schwiderski 2000). New epigraphic material relevant for comparative purposes has become available (e.g., Fales 1996; Gropp 2001). The present edition takes into account these new publications, resulting in a number of new readings of the original text of the letters and some new interpretations of their meaning. (Pardee 2002 arrived too late to be fully integrated into this volume, beyond citing his evaluation of the authenticity of texts 50a and 50b; see ch. 6 note e.)

In general intent the book (in both its original and revised editions) is similar to Edward Wente, *Letters from Ancient Egypt* (SBLWAW 1). There is a significant difference between that volume and this one, however, as regards the question of cultural coherence. Egypt was a highly integrated society, complex but coherent throughout its millennia-long history. The phrase "Egyptian culture" means something we can define. The same is true of ancient "Hebrew culture," the milieu of the letters in chapters 6–7. These Hebrew letters, in fact, were written in the space of a single generation, by Jewish correspondents most of whom lived in southern Judah only a few miles from each other. The case of the Aramaic letters—nearly three-quarters of this collection—is quite different. No such underlying cultural unity exists, despite the fact that the Aramaic correspondence covers a much shorter time span than the Egyptian, some 250 years as opposed to nearly fifteen hundred. "Aramean culture" can be defined in terms of inscriptions and archaeological remains, to be sure. However, that tells us almost nothing about the cultural background of the people who wrote the letters, because few if any of those people were native Arameans.

Throughout much of the first millennium, Aramaic, a Semitic language kin to Hebrew and written in a similar alphabetic script, was the dominant language of cross-cultural communication in the Near East. Like Akkadian (Assyrian and Babylonian) in the second millennium and Greek in the Hellenistic age, Aramaic became an international *lingua franca*. From Egypt to Turkey, across Syria and Mesopotamia, even as far away as Pakistan, Aramaic was used for governmental, commercial, and personal purposes.

The earliest reliable historical references to Arameans date from the time of Tiglath-pileser I of Assyria (1115–1077 B.C.E.). His annals relate that he fought with Arameans along the Euphrates west of Babylonia and in the Syrian desert. Arameans appear sporadically in Assyrian and Babylonian texts throughout the succeeding two centuries, sometimes as friendly tribespeople, sometimes as hostile "people of the steppe."

In the eighth century B.C.E., when Assyria was the dominant imperial power in the Near East, Arameans were widely dispersed among the other population groups of Mesopotamia. By this time Aramaic was beginning to supplant Akkadian as the dominant spoken language in Mesopotamia. Akkadian remained the official language of the empire, but Aramaic was generally used for diplomatic purposes. By the end of the seventh century, the newly established Babylonian Empire was ruled by Aramaic-speaking Chaldeans from southern Iraq. Their successors, the Persians (550–331 B.C.E.), used a number of languages for official purposes, but for general diplomatic and administrative communication, especially with the western part of their empire, Aramaic was the language of choice.

As early as 700 B.C.E., a fairly standardized written form of Aramaic had developed, now known as "Official" or "Imperial" Aramaic. Under Persian auspices, Official Aramaic was taught all across the empire to scribes whose mother tongues ranged from Elamite in the east to Egyptian in the southwest. In addition to this learned scribal usage, a number of dialects of spoken Aramaic were in use in different regions of Mesopotamia, Syria, Palestine, and Egypt.[a]

Under such conditions, it is hardly to be expected that the written language would be uniform. In word formation, vocabulary, and syntax, almost every group of Aramaic texts shows differences, some of them quite pronounced, from other groups. There is a distinct Mesopotamian dialect, for instance (letter no. 1). The Persian administrative correspondence (ch. 5 below) is written in a stilted style full of Persian loanwords.

The closest thing to a common thread in these letters is that of Jewish cultural identity, which links the Aramaic letters in chapters 3–4 to the Hebrew ones in chapters 6–7. But even here, the cultural differences are great: on the one hand, preexilic Palestinian Jews (chs. 6–7); on the other, an isolated postexilic Diaspora community (chs. 3–4).

Unlike Wente's volume, but like several of the subsequently published works in this series, the present volume includes texts in the original languages, transcribed into unvocalized square script. This should not deter readers who lack knowledge of Hebrew or Aramaic. Neither the translations nor the notes presuppose an ability to read the originals. But the originals are there for the large numbers of readers able to use them. One other volume in the series, *Ugaritic Narrative Poetry* (edited by Simon Parker, SBLWAW 9), similarly included the original texts.

The seventy-nine letters gathered here come primarily from two historical settings: (1) Syria-Palestine just before and during the Babylonian invasions prior to the fall of Judah and Philistia half a century later, and (2) Egypt in the earlier part of the Persian period, approximately 500–400 B.C.E. A small number of texts belong to two other historical settings: Assyria in the midst of the civil war that broke out around 650 B.C.E. (no. 1), and southern Palestine toward the end of the Persian period (nos. 71 and 72). In general, the Aramaic letters appear first, then the Hebrew. The final chapter is more eclectic, including the three Canaanite letters along with a few additional Hebrew fragments and two late texts in Aramaic. Within these groupings, the arrangement is roughly chronological.

II. Epistolary Style and Conventions

The style and conventions of ancient Near Eastern letter writing (including the Greek papyri from Hellenistic Egypt) have been extensively studied for nearly a century. It is beyond the scope of this introduction to attempt a thorough form-critical analysis of the Aramaic, Hebrew, and Canaanite letters. The reader interested in pursuing the subject of epistolography in greater detail may consult the studies of Fitzmyer (1981) and Pardee (1982: 153–64) on epistolary structure and formulas, and Porten (1979; 1980) on the physical details of writing on papyrus and leather. A recent German monograph offers an exhaustive analysis of the Aramaic, Hebrew, and Canaanite letters (Schwiderski 2000). Fitzmyer, Pardee, and Schwiderski include the relevant biblical letters in their analyses, as this volume does not.

A letter can be broadly defined as a written communication sent by one person or a group of people to another person or group. This implies that the persons are separated by sufficient distance to prevent them from communicating orally. Typically, letters contain greetings, instructions, requests, and information.

The content of the letters in this anthology is immensely varied. There are short, informal notes between family members and friends about such commonplace topics as shopping for salt (no. 24), mixing dough (no. 19), and shearing sheep (no. 15). There are postcard-style letters "just to say hello" (e.g., no. 9). There are more extended letters on family finances and commercial ventures (ch. 2). Some contain vivid personal details. Several people have just been arrested (nos. 14 and 40) or released from jail (nos. 7, 31, and 32), one correspondent is recovering from snakebite (no. 7), and another pettishly complains that he does not like the tunic his mother has sent him (no. 5)!

In earlier periods of Egyptian history, the rate of literacy among women was considerably lower than it was among men. Some of the Egyptian letters intended for women have an external address in a man's name, suggesting that the recipients needed to have the letters read to them by a man in the household (Wente 1990: 8–9). In the fifth-century Aramaic family correspondence from Egypt (chs. 2 and 3), several letters are written to women, with no suggestion that the recipients were unable to read them for themselves.

Many of the letters deal with military matters: requests for reinforcements, reports on troop movements and missions carried out, intelligence information, requisitions for rations and men, concerns about morale. Virtually all the letters in chapters 1 and 7 are written by soldiers or concern military affairs. A few touch on religious matters, such as the observance of Sabbath (no. 22), the celebration of Passover and Unleavened Bread (nos. 19, 30), and the events surrounding the destruction of the Jewish temple at Elephantine (nos. 33–36). There are also bureaucratic letters between Persian officials, written in a "rubber-stamp" style in which an earlier letter is quoted and action is briefly authorized (ch. 5).

III. Letter-Writing Materials

Classified according to the materials on which they are written, the letters fall into three groups. First, there are ostraca, letters inked on broken pieces of clay pottery (no. 1; chs. 3, 6–7; nos. 68–69, 71–72). The term is sometimes used broadly to include texts written on limestone flakes, but none of the Aramaic letters are written on this material. Typically, Hebrew and Aramaic ostraca are small, ranging from about half the size of the palm of one's hand to the size of two palms held together, and containing from four to a dozen or more short lines of writing. Sometimes only one side (normally the concave) is inscribed, though many letters continue on the convex side. Occasionally the convex and concave contain two entirely different letters.

Number 1 is an ostracon of unique size, far out of proportion with anything else in the collection. Written on a thick piece of a heavy storage jar, it originally measured about 43 by 60 centimeters (17 inches high by almost 2 feet wide) and contained over twenty long lines, though much of it is now lost. The enormous size of this ostracon is perhaps to be explained from the unusual circumstances of the writer. The other ostraca were all written in towns. In an urban setting, small potsherds could always be found lying about in the streets, and such ostraca were invariably used for writing short notes.[b] For longer correspondence, papyrus and leather were the normal media. Where the author of letter no. 1 was when he wrote is unknown, but he had just returned from assignment in the desolate marshes of southern Babylonia and needed to make a lengthy and important report. He may simply have had no access to a friendly urban center where he could buy leather or papyrus or find a scribe competent to write the letter in cuneiform on a clay tablet.

Leather is the second material used for letters. Although only a dozen letters in this collection are written on leather (ch. 5), this material was widely used in Mesopotamia for writing Aramaic. A common motif in Assyrian military art is a pair of scribes standing side by side recording the results of a campaign. One scribe, who is typically bearded, holds a clay tablet on which he is writing in cuneiform with a stylus. The other, clean shaven, writes with a pen on soft material. The second scribe can only be writing in Aramaic, and the soft material is most probably leather. Akkadian texts of the period refer to "scribes who write on skins" (Driver 1965: 1).

No Aramaic documents on leather have survived in Mesopotamia, but the letters in chapter 5 were written either there or in Persia. The leather is stretched thin and appears to have been carefully prepared for writing. It is sometimes described as "parchment," though whether the term is appropriate is largely a matter of definition. It is hardly comparable in quality to good medieval parchment, though no doubt it was the best available at the time.

The third writing material, papyrus, was extensively used in Egypt from very ancient times. Papyrus was made from specially prepared reeds sliced lengthwise, laid out in a grid of vertical strips covered by horizontal strips, then pressed and polished into sheets. These were glued together twenty at a time to form a roll. Papyrus was the most convenient and relatively inexpensive soft writing material known in antiquity. Aside from the ostraca, all of the Aramaic letters written in Egypt (and no. 2 from Philistia) are written on it. Papyrus may also have been used to a limited extent in Mesopotamia, but no Aramaic papyri have been found there. It could not be made locally, and the difficulty of importing it from Egypt would have kept it from being common.

IV. Writing a Letter

A scribe writing a letter on papyrus followed a standard procedure. He would first take a papyrus roll, ordinarily from 25 to 32 centimeters (about 10 to 13 inches) wide. Holding the roll in a horizontal position, the scribe would roll off a length and cut it into a new sheet of the desired height. The letter would be begun on the *recto,* the side originally inside the roll, where the papyrus fibers run perpendicular to the joins. When the recto was filled, the papyrus would be flipped over top to bottom, and the text continued on the *verso* (upside down relative to the recto). A large space would be left at the bottom of the verso for the external address.

When the letter was completed, it would be turned recto-up and folded upward toward the top in a series of horizontal bands, so that the blank space left at the bottom of the verso could be flapped over and exposed. The address would be written on this space. The letter, now folded into one long narrow strip, would then be folded laterally into quarters or halves (in a few cases, thirds), bound with string, and sealed with a lump of wet clay impressed with the seal of the writer. It was now ready for dispatch.

The process was similar with letters on leather, except that the text would be written entirely on the smooth side of the skin. The hair side, corresponding to the verso of a papyrus, was more difficult to write on because of its rougher texture and would not be inscribed, except for the external address and a docket (see below). For an interesting and very detailed account of the manner of writing and folding letters, and how this knowledge is used in reconstructing damaged documents, see Porten (1979; 1980; with numerous illustrations by Ada Yardeni).

V. The Form of a Letter

In broad outline, the letter has three main parts: an opening, which may include an address and a greeting; a body; and a closing, with certain concluding formulas and additional information. The form of a typical letter may be diagrammed as follows:

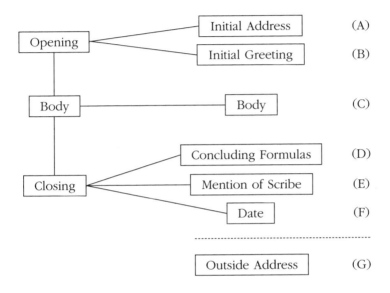

Any of these elements may be omitted. Some letters (e.g., no. 9) consist entirely of greeting formulas with no other message. Other short notes contain only the body, a bare message with no opening or closing formalities (e.g., nos. 12, 23). Let us now examine each of these elements in a little more detail.

A. Initial Address

The first part of the letter is the "initial address," often referred to by the Latin term *praescriptio*. Except for very informal notes, this element is nearly always found in the Aramaic letters. A number of the Hebrew letters from Lachish lack it. The initial address identifies the sender and the recipient. It can be formulated in different ways, with either name coming first, but the most common form is "to A from B." Titles of sender and addressee may be included, especially in more formal correspondence. Such words as "lord," "servant," and terms of family relationship are frequent. In the Hebrew letters there is no formal line between the initial address and the greeting. Instead, there are several formulas incorporating both elements (see below).

Two early Hebrew fragments and the three Canaanite letters all begin with a "double-saying" formula. The basic pattern appears to be, literally translated, "PN (sender) says (as follows): Say to PN (recipient): ... ," and is found with slight variations at the beginnings of nos. 67a:A and B, 68, and 70. (The fragmentary character of no. 67a makes it impossible to determine whether the formula also occurs in it.) A variant form is found in no. 69, in which the names of recipient and sender are found in the opposite order.

The exact literal sense of the "double-saying" phrase is uncertain, because the lack of written vowels makes it impossible to distinguish between the noun "a saying (of)," the indicative verb "he says" (the same consonants may also be read "she says" in Phoenician), and the imperative "say!" But the rendering given above is the most likely. However the words are parsed, the double use of the root word for speech is unlike anything found in the Aramaic correspondence. Whether this distinctive formulation goes back to an old Canaanite model or whether it derives from Akkadian, we do not know. Ugaritic letters from the thirteenth century B.C.E. also use a "double-saying" formula, though it is not identical.

The addresses of the Aramaic letters sometimes use familial language in an honorific sense that does not correspond to the actual relationship of the correspondents; see the similar use of "your brother" and "your son" in two Hebrew letters from Arad (nos. 51, 60). Occasionally, as in several of the Elephantine ostraca, the initial address is omitted. In these cases, we may assume that the letter carrier was given verbal instructions concerning delivery. Characteristically, the word "greetings!" (literally, "peace") follows the names in many of the Aramaic texts.

An additional opening feature is included in most of the letters in chapter 2, also found occasionally in late Babylonian letters. At the very beginning, before the initial address, a "temple greeting" occurs, a word directed to a local shrine in the addressee's town, as for example, "Greetings to the temple of Nabu" (no. 3), "Greetings to the temple of Banit at Syene" (no. 6), "Greetings to the temple of YHW at Elephantine" (no. 10).

B. Initial Greeting

This is a word of greeting, well-wishing, or both. In its simplest form it may consist simply of the word "greetings," as noted above. Sometimes the greetings become elaborate formulas, as in no. 34: "May the God of Heaven bless our lord always, and may he put you in the good graces of King Darius and his household a thousand times more than now. May he grant you long life, and may you always be happy and strong." Between these two extremes, a variety of forms can be found.

Two major types of Aramaic greeting formulas are found. One uses the verb "bless" (e.g., "We bless you by Ptah—may he let us see you again in good health," no. 8); the other uses various phrases with the word "peace," sometimes translated "well-being" or "greetings" depending on context (e.g., "I send you greetings and best wishes for your good health," no. 37). Both types of formula are sometimes found side by side in the same letter.

Many of the Hebrew letters have no greeting formulas. Those that occur are unlike those found in Aramaic. The preferred formula at Lachish uses the verb "hear": "May YHWH send you [literally, 'cause you to hear'] good news this very day" (no. 61; cf. nos. 62–63, 66–67). A variant formula appears in no. 64, where the Hebrew original of the phrase "May YHWH make this time a good one for you" actually uses a form of the verb "see." In nos. 61, 64, and 66, the greeting formula is directly followed by a formula of self-abasement: "I am nothing but a dog." In the Arad letters, a different opening phrase combines the address with a "greeting-plus-blessing" formula: "A sends greetings to [literally, 'sends to greet'] B" followed by "I bless you by YHWH!" (nos. 51, 54, 60). This is once replaced by a simple "To A—May YHWH bless you," (literally, "ask for your peace," no. 55). The Hebrew letter formulas from Kuntillet ʿAjrûd (67a:A and B) have a more elaborate blessing: "I bless you by YHWH of Samaria and his *asherah*," followed by a supplementary blessing in 67a:B: "May he bless you and keep you, and be with my lord." In the Canaanite letters the greeting seems to take the form of a question, "Are you well?" to which the writer of no. 70 adds, "I am." The same question also occurs before the blessings in 67a:B. (On YHWH's *asherah,* see pp. 133–34.)

C. Body

The bodies of the letters are as varied in length and content as are people's motives in writing to each other. One fairly common element is a "secondary greeting," a greeting to be relayed to someone other than the addressee, such as, "Greetings to Shabbetai son of Shug. Greetings to Pasai.... Greetings to the whole neighborhood" (no. 5). Secondary greetings may appear anywhere in the body of the letter, but characteristically they are found at the beginning.

D.–F. Concluding Formulas

Many Aramaic letters have no formal conclusion, and none of the Hebrew or Canaanite ones do. They simply stop when the message is concluded. Some of the Aramaic letters add the concluding sentence "I am sending this letter to greet you" (or "...for your peace of mind," nos. 3–9, 11, 20). The administrative letters in chapter 5 typically record the name of the scribe who wrote the copy (E on the diagram above) and sometimes other persons such as the official who drafted it (no. 40) or persons receiving copies for reference ("so-and-so has been informed...," nos. 38, 41–44). A date (F on the diagram) is not a regular part of Aramaic and

Hebrew letters, but some very formal correspondence is dated (e.g., "the twentieth of Marheshwan, seventeenth year of King Darius," no. 34; cf. no. 49). When a date is given, it usually appears near the end, though in one case it is found after the initial greeting (no. 30).

G. Outside Address

A letter on soft material required an address that could be read from the outside without breaking the seal. Usually the names of both sender and addressee appear, sometimes with slightly different wording and titles from those used inside. Administrative letters (ch. 5) generally add a docket, a brief indication of contents. The Hermopolis papyri (ch. 2) have an additional phrase specifying the location of the addressee, such as, "Let it be carried to Syene."

Despite the lack of cultural homogeneity, there is sufficient commonality in the structure and formulation of these letters to justify our speaking broadly of a common "international" epistolary tradition. In particular, there are similar ways of formulating addresses and greetings that cut across lines of language and historical setting.

VI. Text and Translation Style

The textual bases of this collection are as follows: for the Aramaic papyri (and the documents on leather), the text follows fairly closely that of Porten and Yardeni 1986. In particular, these two scholars are to be credited with joining the two papyrus fragments that comprise no. 32 and with restoring small separated fragments of leather to their proper places in nos. 37, 45, and 47.[c] The degree of dependence on Porten and Yardeni should not be exaggerated, however. Their edition has been collated with earlier editions (especially those of Sachau 1911, Cowley 1923, and Driver 1954, 1965) and with published photographs and, whenever possible, confirmed by examination of the original texts. Notes indicate where my readings differ significantly from those of Porten and Yardeni, but a great many smaller differences remain unnoted, particularly in determining the degree of certainty with which damaged portions of the text can be read or restored.[d]

The Hebrew letters and the Phoenician letter are based on the edition of Pardee 1982, with some revisions following Renz 1995 and others, with the same qualifications as for the Aramaic texts. Other editions consulted are listed in the Sources section at the end of the book.[e]

The readings of the Aramaic ostraca are my own. Originals were examined and new photographs taken whenever possible. Since publication of the first edition of this collection, the new edition of Porten and Yardeni 1999 has appeared. I have accepted some but by no means all of their new readings, as indicated in notes at the appropriate places. These ostraca are extremely difficult to interpret, and the reader who compares the two editions will find numerous differences beyond the obvious ones of style. For the Ammonite and Edomite letters, it is still the case that only preliminary publications are available.

The originals of these letters can be read and in most cases understood reasonably well, but there are limiting factors. Each letter is unique; only one copy exists. (The only exception is no. 34, of which there are two copies.) Thus, when a manuscript is damaged, as many are, there is no parallel textual tradition to which one may turn for help in restoring the gaps.

The most fragmentary letters are barely intelligible, and nearly all of these have been excluded. A few badly damaged letters are included in the collection because of their great intrinsic interest. Number 31, the so-called Passover papyrus, is a significant historical document because of the light it sheds on Jewish ritual observance in the postexilic Diaspora, despite its being so broken and faded that even the word "Passover" has to be restored. The case is similar with the Ashur ostracon (no. 1), the only Aramaic letter from ancient Assyria, and the Adon papyrus (no. 2), which parallels biblical evidence for the Babylonian advance into Syria-Palestine just before Judah and Philistia fell to Nebuchadnezzar. A tiny Hebrew fragment of an ostracon from Arad (no. 52) appears to be a remnant of an accession proclamation of one of the kings of Judah (probably Jehoahaz or Jehoiakim), and an equally fragmentary piece from Lachish (no. 65) bears a tantalizing reference to a certain "[...ya]hu the prophet," a contemporary of Jeremiah.

The accuracy with which missing words can be restored to damaged texts varies a good deal from case to case. Sometimes common epistolary phrases and honorific titles can be restored with confidence. On other occasions, a knowledge of the writers' historical circumstances and the social conventions of the period permits plausible conjectures to be made as to the general content of missing phrases. But in some cases one is reduced to guesswork, trying to make sense of the parts that remain on the basis of an intuitive sense of what *might* have been in the lost passages. Restorations of Aramaic or Hebrew readings are indicated by enclosing the translation in square brackets. A purely conjectural restoration is further indicated by printing the English in italics.

A second limiting factor is vocabulary. For the Hebrew letters, that is only occasionally a problem, but even the earliest Aramaic inscriptions show a mixed vocabulary. Imperial Aramaic was used over many generations in different regions and for different purposes by many persons for whom Aramaic was a second language. Marked dialectical differences among different groups of these letters occur, and we find in them loanwords from a number of different Near Eastern languages.

The Ashur ostracon (no. 1) contains borrowings from Akkadian not found anywhere else in Aramaic. The letters from the Persian chancery (ch. 5) use numerous Persian words, especially administrative titles, but some everyday words as well. The texts from Egypt contain Egyptian loanwords; one letter (no. 49) is so riddled with Egyptian boatyard jargon that we can barely understand it.

Sometimes the meanings of these foreign loanwords are known; sometimes not. Where they are, they are generally translated without comment. Where the sense is uncertain or debated, an explanatory note is added. Where the meaning is unknown, it is indicated by ellipsis or a rough approximation in italics, but the use of brackets, italics, ellipses, and notes has been kept to a bare minimum.

Although the literary level of these letters is not high, they are by no means devoid of color. There are moments of sustained narrative power (the eyewitness narrative of the destruction of the Jewish temple at Elephantine [no. 34]), flashes of wit (Bel-etir's laconic account of his audience with Ashurbanipal, in which the king wryly quotes him a proverb [no. 1]), passages of rhetorical vehemence (Adon's impassioned plea for military aid [no. 2], and the awkward eloquence of a Judean field hand's petition to recover a confiscated garment [no. 50]). There is even some sustained sarcasm, as a subordinate officer at Lachish repeatedly addresses his commander in the most insubordinate manner (no. 64 and especially no. 62).

The style of these translations requires a brief word of explanation, especially since some reviewers who prefer a more literal rendering have raised questions on this point (e.g., Porten 1997). In a word, these are not literal translations. In keeping with the intent of the Writings from the Ancient World series, word order and sentence structure in the translations strive for idiomatic English, even when the Aramaic and Hebrew originals are formulated rather differently. The short, choppy clauses and sentences that characterize some of the originals are often linked to form longer English sentences. Occasionally, long rambling sentences in the original are broken into two or more shorter English sentences. In the new edition, superscript line numbers have been added to the translations to ease the task of comparing the original.[f]

It is characteristic of ancient Semitic style not to spell out the logical and syntactical links that are normally made explicit in European languages. Sometimes these nuances are expressed in the originals by variations in word order; sometimes they are merely implicit. Aramaic and Hebrew frequently form long chains of sentences by repeating a single all-purpose conjunction over and over again. To avoid a monotonous and un-English series of "ands," the ubiquitous conjunction is often omitted in translation. Elsewhere its presence is indicated by any of several English words or by various subordinating and coordinating constructions.

Aramaic and Hebrew writers often use the expression "now" or "and now" to begin a new section of a letter or to introduce a new topic, where in English this is indicated by beginning a new paragraph, or in some cases by starting a new sentence within the same paragraph. Some of the Aramaic letters use demonstrative pronouns much more frequently than is normal in English: for example, "these soldiers," where we would say "the soldiers"; "that Vidranga," where English style prefers simply "Vidranga." In these cases, common English usage has been followed.

The words "your servant" and "my lord" present a special problem. These words belong to the stylized conventions of ancient Near Eastern letter writing and sometimes appear repeatedly throughout a letter. Often the translations reproduce the clichés only where they first occur, thereafter substituting "I" and "you." In a few cases, however, the formulas are repeated in English each time they appear.

The choice was made in each instance on the basis of the translator's sense of the tone of the letter. Where it is a simple matter of the normal conventions of address by an inferior to a superior, using the formula once in the translation suffices. A more obsequious tone, as in no. 50, is reflected by repeating the English phrases each time they occur in the original. Where the writer is being ironic or sarcastic, as in no. 62, one is even tempted to place the words "your servant" in quotation marks. The reader may contrast the rendering of the "servant-lord" formulas in the Adon letter (no. 2) and the Yavneh-Yam petition (no. 50) on the one hand, and the Lachish letters (ch. 7) on the other. In general, an attempt has been made to match the style of each translation—whether stilted, formal, less formal, casual, or downright colloquial—to the style of the original.

In a few cases, footnotes give a literal rendering of expressions translated more idiomatically in the body of the text. The reader may find them useful and may be interested to see how these turns of phrase are expressed in the original.

Notes

[a] For a comprehensive history of the Aramaic-speaking peoples, see Dion 1997.

[b] An oddity, given the universal presence of broken pieces of pottery in ancient Near Eastern towns, is the fact that some of the ostraca in chapter 3 have been reused. Traces of erased texts can be detected beneath nos. 18 and 25. Such reuse was more common in the case of papyri; see the introduction to chapter 8, on no. 67b.

[c] Porten and Yardeni (1999: 135, 150) have recently restored additional fragments of nos. 37, 39–40, and 42.

[d] An example or two may help illustrate the two different methodologies for the scholar or student who is working with the original texts. In no. 11a, where

Porten and Yardeni read in line 6 טב והן לא כספא הבו, I read, on the basis of the original papyrus: טֹֹב וֹהֹן לא כספא הבו. Or again in line 8, where they have באלפֿא], I have the more conservative reading [בֿאֹלֿפֿאֹ]. In general, I find they express a degree of confidence in their reading of damaged passages that I cannot always share. Yardeni's hand copies are of extremely high caliber, but they are interpretations and are no substitute for examination of the originals and of high-quality photographs.

   [e] In no. 62, I have followed the text proposed by Cross 1985, which is based on a number of early photographs of the ostracon, some of them unpublished.

   [f] Because the natural word order in English is so different from that of the Semitic languages, it has often been necessary to indicate only an approximate correlation between the two.

Translations

I

Aramaic Diplomatic-Military Correspondence

THESE LETTERS, WHICH MAY BE broadly defined as diplomatic and military, have little in common beyond the fact that both date from the seventh century. Number 1 comes from mid-seventh-century Assyria. Number 2, from the end of that century, was written from Palestine to Egypt. The correspondents are persons of different status: army officers in the former case, kings in the latter. Even the materials on which the two letters are written are different: potsherd and papyrus, respectively.

Letter no. 1 is unique. The number of letters surviving from this period in Assyrian history runs into the thousands, and they are written in Akkadian, in the Neo-Assyrian dialect. This letter is the only one yet found in Aramaic. It was written with pen and ink on a very large ostracon, a piece of a broken storage jar. Discovered at the site of ancient Ashur during the German excavations of 1903–13, the text is in a poor state of preservation. It was found broken into six fragments with some portions missing. An entire piece of the left margin is completely lost. The effects of groundwater and chemicals have left parts of the remaining surface illegible. Comparison of the original now with photographs taken at the beginning of the 1920s (Lidzbarski 1921) shows that the ink has faded considerably in the interim.

To reconstruct a text that is even partly coherent requires more extensive conjecture than is the rule elsewhere in this volume. Insofar as possible, restorations are based on known phraseology from Neo-Assyrian documents and other Aramaic letters, taking account of the physical length of the lacunae. But those Neo-Assyrian texts are in a different language, and the other Aramaic letters (with the exception of no. 2) are from well over a century later. Thus, the level of uncertainty in the translation of letter no. 1 is high.

This letter was written on the eve of the outbreak of a major civil con-
flict in Mesopotamia. During the reign of King Esarhaddon of Assyria
(680–669 B.C.E.), Assyrian hegemony over Babylonia was firmly established. Babylonia had once been a great independent nation, and there
was still a strong undercurrent of separatist sentiment.[a]

To head off the prospect of Babylonian secession at his death,
Esarhaddon contrived an unusual plan. Against the advice of some of his
counselors, he designated two sons as crown princes: Ashurbanipal was
to succeed him on the Assyrian throne in Nineveh, but Shamash-shum-
ukin was to be "king" in Babylon. We do not know which brother was
the elder; there is some evidence that they may have been twins
(Wiseman 1958: 7; Kaufman 1974: 106). In real terms, the arrangement
meant that Ashurbanipal was imperial ruler of Assyria. Shamash-shum-
ukin, though not technically his brother's vassal, was the junior partner,
little more than a military governor. Thus the fiction of a "king" in
Babylonia was maintained.

Esarhaddon's vassals were required to swear loyalty oaths to him, call-
ing down curses upon themselves if they should ever rebel. Shamash-shum-
ukin did not himself have to swear fealty but was present at the ceremony.

For nearly eighteen years after Esarhaddon's death, the arrangement
worked. Yet Babylonian nationalism was on the rise in the southern cities.
At the same time, dissident Aramean (Chaldean) tribes in southern
Babylonia were becoming more and more restive. Foremost among them
was Bit-Amukkani, a tribe that lived in the marshy hinterland south of the
city of Babylon. The Aramean marsh- and desert-dwellers and the urban
Babylonian nationalists had little in common culturally but were able to
join forces on one key point: opposition to Assyrian rule.

In 651 B.C.E., open war broke out between Assyria and Babylonia,
with Shamash-shum-ukin leading the combined rebel forces in the south.
Hostilities lasted until 648, when the Assyrians regained the upper hand.
In that year, Shamash-shum-ukin and the remnants of his army were
blockaded in Babylon and reduced to starvation. In the closing days of
the siege, the palace was set afire, and Shamash-shum-ukin perished in
the blaze, possibly by his own hand. (The complex course of the war has
been studied exhaustively by Dietrich [1970]; for a shorter summary, see
Saggs 1968: 138–41.)

Letter no. 1 appears to date from just before the outbreak of war in
651. The situation in Babylonia is already unstable. Shamash-shum-ukin
has not yet broken openly with Assyria but has opened secret negotiations
with the tribal leaders of Bit-Amukkani, seeking their support.

The reconstructed letter is a report from an Assyrian officer named
Bel-etir to a fellow-officer, Pir-amurri, who is evidently in the Assyrian
city of Ashur. Both men are loyal to Ashurbanipal and have served

together in the past. Bel-etir has been on special assignment in southern Babylonia tracking small groups of rebel Assyrian soldiers who are serving as couriers in the clandestine negotiations between Shamash-shum-ukin and Bit-Amukkani.

Bel-etir reports a substantial intelligence coup: he has captured four messengers in the remote desert and discovered that they were carrying a letter implicating Shamash-shum-ukin in the incipient uprising. What follows is only partly intelligible, but there seems to be a reference to a fifth conspirator who was captured separately. The prisoners were taken by Bel-etir to Ashurbanipal at an unknown location somewhere in the south.

The captives' ordeal is described in detail. They were publicly humiliated by being tied up with the dogs in the town square (cf. the curse pronounced on Vidranga in no. 34). They were then branded, interrogated, and turned over to Bel-etir as slaves. Bel-etir summarizes the evidence against them: they were caught in rebel territory (prima facie confirmation of their guilt); the brands on their arms were there to see; and they confessed to having gone over to the anti-Assyrian opposition. An additional piece of evidence mentioned is a letter from the first four prisoners to a certain Abbaya, a rebel leader in the far south. Whether this is the confiscated letter already mentioned or a second one is unclear.

The rebels, possibly destined for eventual execution, seem to have been given a reprieve through a surprise action by another officer. A certain Upaqa-ana-arbail, without Bel-etir's knowledge and for unstated reasons, has had some of the men transported north to Ashur. Perhaps he was simply an overzealous subordinate who wished to have them interrogated at army headquarters. Bel-etir orders curtly that they be sent back at once. Expecting opposition from someone named Apil-esharra, perhaps Upaqa-ana-arbail's superior at Ashur, Bel-etir observes that the prisoners themselves can be made to confirm his story.

A fourth officer, Naid-Marduk, is being sent by Bel-etir to Ashur to overtake the prisoner convoy and bring them back. Several additional names are mentioned of persons who are to be returned to Babylonia. Again the reasons are not given. They may be rebels from Assyria's northern possessions, being sent south into exile or for public execution.

There follows a stylized list of four successive Assyrian rulers who exiled persons from various places, followed by a badly broken passage referring to the punishment of traitors. The meaning of the words translated "burn" and "burning" is uncertain, but they may allude to a widely attested ancient Near Eastern curse directed against a rebellious vassal: death by fire. If so, this part of the letter, with its solemn style, list of royal precedents, and references to treaty curses, is a virtual death sentence for the prisoners in question. Little is clear in the final lines, except that someone is angry with the writer and that something is said about a place called Bit-Dibla.

Half a century separates this letter from no. 2. During the interim, major upheavals occurred in Near Eastern politics. By the end of the seventh century, Assyria had collapsed and Babylonia was now the ascendant power. The Neo-Babylonian Empire was flourishing under the recently instituted kingship of the Chaldeans, descendants of the same south Babylonian tribes who had supported Shamash-shum-ukin's abortive war of independence.

The new military leader was Nebuchadnezzar. In 605 while still crown prince, Nebuchadnezzar defeated the Egyptian armies at Carchemish and Hamath in Syria. By 604, now sole ruler in Babylonia after the death of his father Nabopolassar, he was again on the march, aiming to extend Babylonian influence down the Syro-Palestinian coast to the Egyptian border. The events of these years are well documented, both in the Babylonian Chronicle (Wiseman 1956) and the Hebrew Bible (especially 2 Kgs 24:1–7 and Jer 46–47).

Letter no. 2 was written in the midst of this chaotic situation by one Adon, ruler of one of the coastal city-states lying in Nebuchadnezzar's path, probably Ekron (Porten 1981). In great consternation he appeals to his overlord, the Egyptian pharaoh Neco II (610–594), for military aid, reminding the Egyptian that he, Adon, has been a faithful vassal and as such is entitled to support.

The letter reached its destination. The papyrus, found at Saqqara, bears a notation in demotic (a cursive form of Egyptian) jotted by an Egyptian file clerk. The appeal, however, was to no avail. Neco was in no position to help his desperate vassal. There were no auxiliary troops to send, and within short order all of the coastal cities were forced to capitulate to the Babylonian army.

Report of an Assyrian Officer

1. Ashur Ostracon (Berlin, St. Mus. VA 8384) [†]
(Ashur, ca. 650 B.C.E.)

|אל א|חי פרור אחוך בלטר שלם לש|לחת עלי מן זין| 1

|הוית| עמי את במתכדי ואנה וערבי ומ|... אתן בית| 2

|אוכן אזי אזל|ת מן ארך עם גרצפן ועם וגמ̇ר א|......| 3

אנה |רדף קרקן ב|בית אוכן 4 המו אגרת מלך בבל |הות| 4

[†] The sign ?←... indicates a lacuna of uncertain length at the left edge of a column.

בידו֯ה֯י֯יה֯ם יה֯עבדן מרד ב֯בית אוכן בחפירו במדברא אחזן 5
המן֯ [......]

איתו֯ית֯ן / המן֯ ..... ואנגרתא ה֯ו֯שרת למרי מלכא אזי ו֯גבר֯ן אחזן 6
מן נֹה֯ [....]

ואחית ו֯עם כלהם֯ קֹדם ו֯מראֹי מֹל֯כֹא בארדחן עם כלביא שמן 7
יהב המו לי מראֹי מֹלכֹא֯ עבדן

כי / זא ו֯זאן אמר לי מראֹי מלכא לאמר ו֯זלֹך֯ן המו ולטחנו לה 8
יטעם / כֹא חזית ב֯ו֯עניֹן זילי מן֯

בית אוכן המו ידיהם כתבת וקימת קֹדמי קֹו֯ם֯ קרקן הלֹו בבית 9
אוכן / המו מן יֹדו֯הֹו֯י֯הם אחזת אנגרת֯

אבֹי יֹאמֹר לאמר מן שמהיקר ו֯נֹבוזרכן אחשֹו֯ין וֹלֹול נבוזרכן 10
ואחשׁי אפֹקנרבֹיל שם ו֯במֹסֹגֹר ב֯[....]

וֹלֹול שמהיקֹר ואבֹי הלֹו הֹו֯ש֯ר֯ כֹזֹי יֹאֹתֹה אֹפֹקנֹרבֹיל אֹשׁור מן 11
עקב יהֹתֹב המו לֹאֹפֹק֯[.....→?] והן֯

פלסֹר ו֯ישׁ֯אֹל הֹצֹדֹא הנֹי מלֹיֹא אֹלֹה בֹ֯לֹטֹרֹ֯ן שׁמֹי כֹתֹב עֹל 12
יֹדֹהֹיֹהֹם וקֹרֹא הֹמֹוֹ שׁאֹל / הֹמֹוֹ הֹצֹדֹֹ֯אֹ[.....→?]

[..]אֹ אֹלֹה הֹלֹו֯ן עבֹדן / הֹמוֹ / זֹלֹי קֹרֹקֹן הֹלֹוֹ [..עֹם֯] זֹי / בֹיֹת / 13
אֹוֹכֹן / הֹמֹוֹ הֹלֹוֹ נֹדֹמֹרֹדֹך עֹזֹרֹך שׁלֹחֹתֹ / קֹֹ֯דֹמֹ֯יֹהֹם [.....→?]

ו֯תֹהֹתֹבֹ֯ הֹמֹוֹ אֹחֹזֹא הֹמֹוֹ הֹוֹשׁרֹ / לֹן אֹזֹי בֹר / נֹמֹ֯לֹ[...]בֹן וֹבֹר 14
בֹ[...]וֹֹבֹן זֹבֹנֹאֹדֹן וֹנֹבוֹשׁלֹם זֹי בֹיֹת עֹדֹן אֹזֹי [.→?]

[.....]עֹ֯ שׁבֹ֯י שׁבֹה תֹכֹלֹתֹפֹלֹסֹר מֹן בֹיֹת / אֹו֯כֹן ו֯ושׁבֹין שׁבֹה אֹלֹלֹי 15
מֹ֯ן בֹיֹת עֹדֹן ושׁבֹי שׁבֹה שׁרֹכֹן מֹן דֹרֹסֹן

ושׁבֹו֯י שׁבֹה סֹנֹ֯חֹרֹב מֹן כֹשׁדֹ֯ [...מֹלֹכֹין אֹשׁוֹ֯ר יֹגֹזֹ֯לֹן .....] מֹן שֹׁנֹ֯ה 16
יֹקֹרֹקֹן ויֹכֹסֹאֹן / הֹמֹו וֹכֹימֹן מֹלֹכֹי אֹ֯שׁוֹר [.....]

בֹ[.]דֹיֹבֹ[... יֹאֹמֹרֹן֯] לאֹמֹר קֹרֹקֹי אֹל תֹחֹזֹו מֹן[..][.כֹ. ....][.] אֹשׁוֹ֯ר 17
אֹשׁה אֹכֹלֹתֹהֹם וֹמֹראֹי מֹלֹכֹא פֹקֹדֹ [.....]

לֹמֹ[.]נֹדֹא אֹ[.....][...] קֹרֹקֹי אֹשׁוֹר יֹכֹסֹאֹן 18

לֹנֹבֹוֹזֹרֹשׁבֹשׁ וֹ[...]אֹרֹה מֹלֹאֹכֹתֹי אֹשׁלֹחֹ לֹך הֹלֹבֹתֹי מֹלֹא אֹת לֹבֹת 19
אֹלֹהֹא זֹי [.]טֹי[.][.....] וֹֹגֹ[.............]

לֹמֹה לֹבֹתֹי מֹלֹא [...] וֹכֹעֹתֹ[....] אֹפֹיֹא בֹ[..][.ק.........]אֹ֯פֹיֹא 20
כֹזֹי תֹחֹזֹה וֹֹיֹאֹ[..] שׁנֹה שׁלֹחֹנֹֹ֯ה [......]

בֹבֹית / דֹבֹלֹא לֹ[..][.]וֹ שׁ֯וֹ֯רֹן ה֯[.][.] זֹי הֹמֹרֹתֹכֹ[.] זֹי 21
אֹת[.......] שׁוֹרֹן זֹי בֹיֹת דֹבֹלֹא

[1]To my brother Pir-amurri from your brother Bel-etir:
Greetings [...].

[You have not written to me since] [2]you were with me in Babylonia. I and Arbayya and [... went to Bit-[3]Amukkani. Then] you [left] Uruk with Ger-sapun and ...[b] [...].

[4]I [was chasing defectors[c] in] Bit-Amukkani. There were four of them. They had in their possession a letter from the king of Babylon (Shamash-shum-ukin) [5]and were trying to stir up a rebellion in Bit-Amukkani. We captured them at Hapiru in the desert. [6][Then] I brought them [to ...] and sent [the letter] to my lord the king (Ashurbanipal). Then we captured [a man from ...], [7]and I took [them all][d] before my lord the king [in fetters].

They were put with the dogs.[e] My lord the king gave them to me [as slaves]. [8]For this is what my lord the king said to me, "They are [yours]! As the saying goes, 'They have ground it; now let them eat it!'"[f]

This is what I have seen [with my own eyes]: They [are from] [9]Bit-Amukkani. Their arms are inscribed, and they swore an oath in my presence that they had indeed defected. They were, after all, in Bit-Amukkani! [I also confiscated] from them [a letter to] [10]Abbaya that said, "From Shemeh-yeqar, Nabu-zer-ukin, and Ahishay and Walwal(?)."

Upaqa-ana-arbail has put Nabu-zer-ukin and Ahishay [in prison in ...], [11]but now I find that he [has had] Walwal(?), Shemeh-yeqar, and Abbaya [taken away]. When Upaqa-ana-arbail arrives in Ashur, he is to return them immediately to Apqu [...]. If [12]Apil-esharra asks, "Is this report true?" my name "Bel-etir" is inscribed on their arms. Call them in and ask them whether it is true: [...] [13][...] Are they my slaves? Did they defect? Were they with the men from Bit-Amukkani?

I have sent your adjutant Naid-Marduk on ahead of them[g] [...]. [14]Send them back; I must deal with them! In addition, send us Bar-[...][h] and Bar-[...]-zabina, Zaban-iddina and Nabu-ushallim of Bit-Adini. Then [...].

[15]Tiglath-pileser exiled prisoners from Bit-Amukkani,
Ululai (Shalmaneser V) exiled [prisoners] from Bit-Adini,
Sargon exiled prisoners from Dur-Sin,
[16]Sennacherib exiled prisoners from Chaldea(?),[i]

[... the kings of] Assyria would [seize them ...]. Whenever(?) anyone defected, they would seize them, and burn(?) them. The kings of Assyria would always [...] [17][... and] would say, "Let there be no defectors from me; may a fire devour them! My lord the king has given orders [*that they are indeed to be put to death...*] [18][...] fugitives from Assyria are to be burned(?).

[19]As for Nabu-zer-ushabshi and [...]: I will be sending you my report. Are you really in such a god-awful rage at me that [...]? [20]Why are you so angry at me?

Now [...]

When you see [...], we sent [...] ²¹at Bit-Dibla [...]-shum-iddina of Bit-Dibla.

Appeal to Pharaoh for Military Aid

2. Adon Papyrus (Cairo, Eg. Mus. J. 86984 = 3483)
(Saqqara, ca. 604 B.C.E.)

A

אל מרא מלכן פרעה עבדך אדן מלך עֹ[קרן שלם מרא מלכן 1
פרעה אלהין

שמיא וארקא ובעל שמין אלה[א רבא ישאלו שגא בכל עדן 2
ויהארכו יומי[ן

פרעה כיומי שמין רֹמין זֹי[......].............. חילא[ן 3

זֹי מלך בבל אתו מטאֹו אפק וֹעֹ[......................] 4

[....] אחזו וֹיֹבלו [.....] בכל[......................] 5

כי מרא מלכן פרעה ידע כי עבדך[......................] 6

למשלח חיל להצלתני אֹל יֹשבקני כי לא שקר עבדך בעדי 7
מרא מלכ[ן

ושבתה עבדך נצר ונגדא זנה [......................] 8

פחה במתא וספר שנדור סנ[......................] 9

B

<demotic>   10

¹To Pharaoh, Lord of Kings, from your servant King Adon of [Ekron.

May the gods of] ²heaven and earth and Beel-shemayn [the great] god [seek abundantly at all times the welfare of my lord Pharaoh, Lord of Kings. May they grant] ³Pharaoh [days as long] as the days of the high heavens!ⁱ

[...The army] ⁴of the king of Babylonia has come. They have advanced as far as Aphek, and [...]. ⁵They have captured [...] and have brought [...], in all [...].

[...] ⁶for Pharaoh, the Lord of Kings knows that your servant [...] ⁷to send troops to rescue me. Do not abandon [me, for your servant has not violated the treaty of the Lord of Kings:] ⁸your servant has been faithful to his treaty obligations.

Now this commander [...] [9]a governor in the land. As for the letter of Sin-duri(?), [...].
[10]Demotic notation: What the ruler of Ekron(?)[k] gave to [...].

Notes

[a] The last great Babylonian ruler prior to the period under discussion had been the warrior-king Nebuchadnezzar I (1124–1103 B.C.E.). After a long period of instability in Mesopotamia, the Assyrians became the dominant power in the region under the leadership of Tiglath-pileser III (744–727 B.C.E.), who is mentioned in text no. 1 (line 15).

[b] The name written consonantally as "WGMR" is not known.

[c] Literally, "fugitives, runaways," this word refers to persons stirring up rebellion against Assyrian hegemony in Babylonia.

[d] Literally, "I went with them before the lord my king in fetters." Since that could not apply to Bel-etir himself, the verb should perhaps be emended to a causative form.

[e] Or perhaps "auxiliary troops" (Fales 1987, 468–69).

[f] "As the saying goes" is implied. The words that follow appear to be a popular proverb equivalent to "They've made their bed; now let them lie on it!"

[g] Or "to you."

[h] Evidently a personal name beginning with the Aramaic word "son of." Lemaire and Durand (1984: 52) discuss this as a distinctive form of dynastic name found among the Aramaic peoples of Syria.

[i] Or "Kush."

[j] Or (with a different reading of the first letter of the last word) "as the days of the heavens and the waters" (Porten and Yardeni 1986: 6).

[k] Ekron is plausible, both graphically and historically (Porten 1981: 43–45).

II

Business and Family Letters

ALL BUT ONE OF THE papyrus letters in this chapter belong to two small collections of family correspondence that deal with a mixture of personal and business matters. The first group is known as the Hermopolis papyri, after the site where they were discovered in 1945, the ancient Hermopolis Magna (modern Tuna el-Gebel), on the west bank of the Nile about 240 kilometers (150 mi.) south of Memphis. Six of the seven letters in this group (nos. 3–8) were dispatched by three men residing in Memphis, all belonging to the same family. The addressees are relatives in the south, in Syene (modern Aswan) and Luxor. These letters were all penned by the same scribe and were found still tied and sealed with the same seal. Something happened to the courier en route; the letters were never delivered. Number 9, from a different sender, is also addressed to Luxor.

The Hermopolis letters are not internally dated, but the script, which is more archaic than that of the Elephantine letters (chs. 3–4), suggests a date around the end of the sixth century. Some features of the Aramaic are archaic; others are innovative. Still others are reminiscent of a Canaanite language such as Phoenician. This may indicate a scribe not fully conversant with literary Aramaic, or it may simply reflect a Lower Egyptian regional dialect.

The letters concern family commercial activities. There are frequent references to the purchase and shipment of goods: olive oil, castor oil, perfume, lumber, wool, cloth, leather, and various articles of clothing. Castor oil, produced in the south, had a particularly high trade value. Members of the Memphis branch of the family repeatedly ask their relatives in Syene and Luxor for shipments of it.

Letters 6 and 7 outline a complex financial transaction involving relatives in all three cities. The background can be tentatively reconstructed as follows: Makkebanit, his kinsman Banitsar, and the latter's son are in Memphis; Banitsar's mother, Tabi, is in Luxor; Tashai, Makkebanit's sister, is in Syene. Banitsar and his son have been arrested and imprisoned for debt. Makkebanit has redeemed them; that is, he paid the debt in order to secure their release. In exchange, Banitsar wrote his benefactor an I.O.U. for the amount of the debt. The two letters seek the help of other family members in paying off the debt. Tabi is asked to pay a share of her son's obligation to Makkebanit by sending an equivalent value of wool to Makkebanit's sister in Syene. Makkebanit writes to Tashai in Syene (no. 6), while Banitsar writes his mother in Luxor (no. 7), describing how the transaction is to take place (Porten and Greenfield 1974; Hillers 1979).

The second group of family letters (nos. 10 and 11) is known as the Padua papyri, after the Civic Museum in Padua, where they are now located. They date from the fifth century, but no. 10 is perhaps a generation older than no. 11. The exact Egyptian provenance of the two letters is not known, though we may conjecture that they were found at Elephantine.

Number 10 was written by one Oshea, a Jewish resident of Migdol in the eastern Delta, to his son Shelomam, who is travelling in Upper Egypt. The letter was dispatched to Elephantine, to be held for the son's arrival. Apparently Shelomam is entitled to a government salary, perhaps because he and his associates are soldiers assigned to caravan escort duty (Porten 1968: 42). The local government office at Migdol has refused to pay Shelomam's salary while he is away, and Oshea has evidently arranged to have the money held until the young man gets back. The damaged middle of the letter alludes to some household misfortune. Oshea informs his son that it is not serious and that Shelomam should not be overly upset by it. The final section reports on several articles of clothing destined for various family members.

Number 11 is a fragment of a letter written by a young man to an older woman. He mentions a lawsuit involving a certain Pakhnum and urges his correspondent to give money to this person, but the details are lost. The letter concludes with personal greetings.

The last letter in the chapter, no. 11a, does not belong to either of these two family collections. It is a business letter concerning commerce and shipping on the Nile. The background circumstances can be deduced by reading between the lines. In this case, the situation is somewhat involved.

Two men with Persian names, Spentadata and Armatidata, probably administrators in the government bureaucracy or military officers, are co-owners of a boat used in the Nile trade. The partners employ two Egyptian men, Hori and Petemahu, who double as crew and purchasing agents. The Egyptians have been given money by Spentadata, writer of the letter, to purchase grain along the way to an unnamed destination.

After the first few sentences, the letter is structured in a haphazard manner that modern interpreters have found confusing, but it appears that the circumstances are as follows. Spentadata has no way of knowing whether or not the two sailors have been able to buy any grain and, if so, whether they have resold any of the cargo at a profit. So he gives them a series of instructions covering different eventualities: (1) if you have bought grain for us, ship my share back to me; (2) if you have sold any, turn my share of the profit over to Armatidata; (3) if you have not bought any grain, turn over the money to Armatidata, who will take care of the necessary purchasing and shipping; (4) if any grain is still left over after the various consignments are delivered, give it to Armatidata so he can resell it. In any case, follow Armatidata's orders. Finally (this part is addressed to Hori alone),[a] keep an eye on Petemahu, possibly a slave, so he does not run away.

In all of these letters there is considerable ambiguity in the use of familial designations such as "mother," "sister," and "brother." Sometimes the words have their ordinary meaning. At other times they are used as honorific or generic titles to address relatives, but without intending to specify the actual relationship. A case in point is no. 9, whose initial address "to my mother Atardimri from your brother Ami" would be nonsense if taken literally. On the outside address of this letter, Ami refers to the same woman as "my sister." Similarly, no. 10 is addressed "to my son Shelomam from your brother Oshea" (outside address: "to my brother Shelomam son of Oshea from your brother Oshea"). In no. 7, we find Tabi addressed as Banitsar's "mother" in the outside address but as his "sister" in the letter proper. Number 11 uses "mother-son" language in the greeting, but a different woman, Menahemet, is identified by the writer as "my mother" in line 5. "Mama" (nos. 4–5) is a personal name or nickname. Clearly the "brothers" in no. 11a are business partners, not relatives.

Further confusion is introduced by the occasional practice of using alternative name forms for the same person, such as Nabushezib-Nabusha (no. 5; cf. nos. 6 and 7) and Atardimri-Atardi (no. 9). Another kind of ambiguity occurs where the formal terms "your servant" and "my lord" are used among family members, as in no. 4. Frequently it is unclear whether the language of family relationship is to be taken literally, and we are unsure of the true relationship of the persons so named. Probably some of the other Aramaic letters also follow this ambiguous practice. In many cases, we are not well enough informed to judge.

Nearly all the letters in this chapter include a distinctive "temple greeting" formula, directed to sanctuaries located where the recipients live. The Hermopolis letters include greetings to temples of Nabu (no. 3), Banit (nos. 4 and 6), Bethel (no. 5), and "the Queen of Heaven" (no. 5) at Syene. Number 10 has a corresponding greeting to the temple of YHW at Elephantine. (The fact that the Jews of Elephantine had their own temple was only one of a number of significant ways in which they differed from their more rigorous contemporaries in Israel. This temple and its destruction becomes the focus of a series of letters in chapter 4 [nos. 33–36].)[b] In addition to the temple greeting, most of the Hermopolis letters (nos. 3–8) include a blessing in the name of Ptah, the chief divinity of Memphis, where the senders live.

The letters in chapters 2–5 come from the period when the kings of Persia dominated the ancient Near East. A sketch of this era, focusing on the satrapy of Egypt, with which most of the letters are associated, helps place them in their proper historical and social setting. Reference is made in other chapters to the satrapies of Abar-Nahara ("across the river"), the huge trans-Euphrates region to which Judah and Samaria belonged, and Babylonia, originally part of a larger district of Mesopotamia and Abar-Nahara that was made into a separate administrative area by Darius I in 516 B.C.E.

Cyrus the Great (550–530 B.C.E.) was the founder of the Persian Empire, known as the "Achaemenid" Empire after the name of Achaemenes, the traditional ancestor of the ruling house. Cyrus's reputation rested on his conquests; we know little about how he administered his realm. His son and successor, Cambyses (529–522), brought Egypt into the empire, but he died within a few years during a series of revolts in which various pretenders tried to seize the throne.

Darius I (521–486) had to spend his first two years reestablishing order, as he recounts in his famous trilingual inscription at Behistun. According to Herodotus (*History* 3.90–97), Darius organized the administration of the empire into twenty satrapies, of which Egypt was the sixth. The Behistun inscription lists twenty-two subject lands, not counting Persia itself.

Two-thirds of the way through Darius's reign (499), the Ionian cities in Asia Minor rebelled. There followed a series of altercations with the Greeks, leading up to Darius's unsuccessful invasion of the Greek mainland, which was brought to an abrupt end by the Persian defeat at Marathon (490). On the accession of Darius's son, Xerxes (486–465), a revolt broke out in Egypt that took some three years to put down. After dealing harshly with a second revolt in Babylonia, Xerxes turned his attention back to Greece. The Greek wars, whose details lie beyond our scope, culminated in the Persian calamities at Salamis (480), Platea, and Samos (479) and ultimately led to a complete Persian withdrawal from Europe.

Although these events involved Egypt only peripherally, they provide the backdrop for the political instability that was endemic there during the fifth century. Rebellions at the beginning of the reigns of Xerxes and Artaxerxes I (465–424) took years to subdue. In 465, a Libyan named Inaros initiated a revolt, with Athenian support, that almost succeeded. He and his supporters drove the Persian army out of the Delta and placed Memphis under siege before the Persians were able to reestablish control.

Egypt was hardly more stable during the long reign of Darius II (423–404). Insurrections broke out periodically at Elephantine, Thebes, and elsewhere, to which there are repeated allusions in the letters (nos. 32–34, 40, 42–43; there are hints of tension also in nos. 31 and 38). Shortly after the beginning of the reign of Artaxerxes II (404–358), there occurred yet another major revolt in Egypt. This time the Egyptians expelled their Persian suzerains, and they regained independence under native rulers for over half a century, Dynasties Twenty-Eight, Twenty-Nine, and Thirty.

Family Business Letters from Lower Egypt

3. Hermopolis 1 (Cairo Univ., Arch. Mus. P. 1687) (late sixth-early fifth century)

A

1 שלם בית נבו אל אחתי רעיה מן אחכי מכבנת

2 ברכתכי לפתח זי יחזני אפיך בשלם שלם בנתסרל וארי

3 ואסרשת ושרדר חרוץ שאל שלמהן וכעת שלם ⦅ול⦆

4 לחרוץ תנה אל תצפי לה כדי תכלן תעברן לה עבד אנה

5 לה ותפמת ואחתסן מסבלן לה וכעת ארה ספר לה שלחתי

6 בשמה וכעת זי מלתי ˆלבתיˆ לאמר לה שאל על חרוץ כעת

7 ⦃מ⦄>ה<לו כזי עבד אנה לחרוץ כות תעבד בנת עלי

B

8 ארה לא אחי הו חרוץ וכעת הלו יהב להן פרס

9 תנה ויתלקח קדמתהן בסון וכעת הן את ערב עליכי

10 אתיה לתפמת וכעת מדעם אל תזבני בכסת ותשרי לה

11 שלם יקיה הוי שלחת לה וכעת הוי חזית על תשי ועל

12 ברה ושלחי כל טעם זי הוה בב ˆיˆתי לשלמכי שלחת ספר‐

13 ה זנה

14 אל אבי פסמי בר נבונתן מן מכבנת סון יבל

---

[1]Greetings to the temple of Nabu!

To my sister Reia from your brother Makkebanit.

[2]I bless you by Ptah—may he let me see you again in good health!

Greetings to Banitsarli, Uri, [3]Isireshut, and Sardur. Haruz sends greetings to them.

[4]Haruz is all right here. Don't worry about him! I am doing everything for him you could do yourself. [5]Tapamut and Ahat-sin are providing for him.

I understand you haven't written [6]him. Why? Is it that you're angry at me? Do you think, "He isn't looking after Haruz"? [7]May Banit do as well for me as I am doing for Haruz! [8]After all, he's my brother, isn't he?

The others have received their salary [9]here, but it can be drawn on at Syene only in their presence. So if any guarantor makes a claim against you, [10]let him bring it to Tapamut. Don't sell the cloak so you can buy something else—don't let it go![c]

[11]Give my best to Yekia. And do look after Tashai and [12-13]her son. Let me know everything that's happening at home.

I am sending this letter to greet you!

[14]*Address:* To my father Psami son of Nabunetan from Makkebanit. Let it be carried to Syene.

4. Hermopolis 3 (Cairo Univ., Arch. Mus. P. 1689) (late sixth–early fifth century)

A

1	שלם בית בנת בסון על מראי פסמי עבדך מכבנת ברכתך
2	לפתח זי יחזני אפיך בשלם שלם אמי ממה שלם
3	אחי בתי ואנשתה ובנוהי שלם רעיה אל תצף לחרוץ
4	לה שבק אנה לה 1 כדי מטאה ידי וכעת עבד אנה לה
5	אל אחי וחפרע מן אחך מכבנת שלם וחין שלחת לך וכעת
6	הן מטאך סר / חלצה שלח לי ביד עקבה בר וחפרע
7	וכעת כל זי תצבה שלח לי הושר לי משכן
8	מסת לבש משך 1

B

9	והוי לקח שערן מן תשי ויהב בגשרן
10	ושבק כל גשר זי תשכח לממה זבנת חטבת ומשח
11	בשם למתיה לכן ולה אשכחת אש למיתית לכן וכעת
12	תקם יתו לי חפנן 5 אל תצפו לי לכן אנה יצף
13	לשלמכן שלחת {{ל.]}} ספרה זנה

14   אל אבי פסמי מן מכבנת בר פסמי סון יבל

[1]Greetings to the temple of Banit at Syene!
To my lord Psami from your servant Makkebanit.

I bless you [2]by Ptah—may he let me see you again in good health!

Greetings to my mother Mama. Greetings to [3]my brother Beti, his wife and children.

Greetings to Reia. Don't let her worry about Haruz. [4]Insofar as possible, I do not leave him alone. I am also providing for him.

[5]To my brother Wahpre from your brother Makkebanit.

May you live long and well.

[6]If the *pot of new oil*[d] has reached you, send me word by Akba son of Wahpre. [7]Let me know what you need. Send me enough skins [8]for a leather garment. [9]You should be getting some barley from Tashai. Trade it for lumber [10]and store all the lumber you find at Mama's place.

I have bought some striped material and [11]scented oil to send to you, but I haven't yet found anyone to bring them. [12]Please have five small measures of castor oil sent to me.

Don't worry about me; let me worry about you instead! [13]I am sending this letter to greet you.

[14]*Address:* To my father Psami from Makkebanit son of Psami.
Let it be carried to Syene.

5. Hermopolis 4 (Cairo Univ., Arch. Mus. P. 1690) (late sixth–early fifth century)

A

1   שלם בית בתאל ובית מלכת שמין אל אחתי נניחם
2   מן אחכי נבושה ברכתכי לפתח זי יחוני אפיך בשלם
3   שלם ביתאלנתן שלם נכי ועשה ותשי וענתי ואטי ורע׳
4   וכעת מטתני כתנה זי אושרתי לי ואשכחתה שנטת כלה
5   ולבבי לה דבק לה הן חזית מה אתרתן אתננה בתקבה
6   1 לאטי וכעת כתנה זי התתי לי סון הי מלבש
7   אנה וכעת תקם יתו לן ונתנהי במשח וכעת אל
8   תצפי לן לי ולמכבנת לכן אנחן יצפן אזדהרי
9   בביתאלנתן מן חבב וכעת אן אשכחת אש מהימן
10   אתה לכן מדעם שלם שבתי בר שוג שלם פסי

B

11   שלם עדר בר פסי שלם שאל בר פטחרטיס ואשה

12   בר פטחנם שלם סחתה כלה לשלמכן שלחת ספרה

13   זנה שלם אבי פסמי מן עבדך נבושה שלם אמי

14   ממה ‖ו‖שלם אחי בתי ואנשתה שלם וחפרע

15   אל נניחם מן נבושזב בר פטחנם סון

[1]Greetings to the temple of Bethel and the temple of the Queen of Heaven. To my sister Nanaiham [2]from your brother Nabusha.

I bless you by Ptah—may he let me see you again in good health!

[3]Greetings to Bethelnetan. Greetings to Nikkai(?), Asah, Tashai, Anati, Ati, and Reia.

[4]The tunic you sent me has arrived. I found it all streaked;[e] [5]I just don't like it at all! *Do you have plenty of other kinds?*[f] If I knew, I would exchange it for a *dress*[g] [6]for Ati. I do wear the tunic you brought to Syene for me.

[7]Please have some castor oil sent to us, so we can exchange it for olive oil.

Don't [8]worry about me and Makkebanit; let us worry about you instead! Take care of [9]Bethelnetan; keep Habib away from him! If I can find anyone dependable, [10]I will send you something.

Greetings to Shabbetai son of Shug. Greetings to Pasai. [11]Greetings to Eder son of Pasai. Greetings to Sheil son of Petehortais and Asah [12]son of Petekhnum. Greetings to the whole neighborhood.

I am sending this letter to greet you! [13]Greetings to my father Psami from your servant Nabusha. Greetings to my mother [14]Mama. Greetings to my brother Beti and his household. Greetings to Wahpre.

[15]*Address:* To Nanaiham from Nabushezib son of Petekhnum. To Syene.

6. Hermopolis 2 (Cairo Univ., Arch. Mus. P. 1688) (late sixth–early fifth century)

A

1   שלם בית בנת בסון אל אחתי תשי מן אחכי מכבנת

2   ברכתכי לפתח זי יחזני אפיכי בשלם שלם נבושה

3   תנה אל תצפו לה לה מנס אנה לה מן מפי שלם

פסמי יקה שלם נניחם וכעת הלו מסת כספה זי 4

הוה בידי נתתן ופדת לבנתסר בר תבי אחת 5

נבושה כסף ש׳ 6 וזוז כסף זוז וכעת שלחי 6

על תבי ותושר לכי עמר מן קצתה זי כסף ש׳ 1 7

וכעת הן יהב לכי נקיה וגזתה שלחי לי 8

והן יהב לכי עמרה זי על מכי שלחי לי 9

והלה יהב לכי שלחי לי ואקבל עליהן תנה 10

וכעת זבנת משח זית ליקה וכתן ואף לכי תקבת 11

שפרת ואף משח בשם לבת בנת ולעד אשכח 1 12

אש למושרתהם לכן וכעת הושרי לי תקם חפנן 13

והוי יהבת עבר לוחפרע ויהוי זבן גשרן 5 14

ושבק בבתה אל תקמי קדמתה כל גשר זי ישכח 15

יזבן והן יהב לכי רעיה עמר שלחי לי שלם 16

תטסרי אזדהרי בה לשלמכן שלחת ספרה זנה 17

B

אל תשי מן מכבנת בר פסמי סון יבל 18

[1]Greetings to the temple of Banit at Syene!
To my sister Tashai from your brother Makkebanit.

[2]I bless you by Ptah—may he let me see you again in good health!

Nabusha is well [3]here. Do not worry about him. I am not taking him away from Memphis. Greetings [4]to Psami and Yake. Greetings to Nanaiham. The sum of money I [5]had—I have paid it to redeem Banitsar,[h] the son of Nabusha's sister Tabi: [6]6½ silver shekels at the usual rate of conversion.[i] Tell [7]Tabi to send you one shekel's worth of wool as her share of the money. [8]If you are given a lamb to shear, let me know. [9]If you are given the wool owed to me(?), let me know. [10]And if you are not given anything, let me know so I can register a complaint against them here.

[11]I have bought some olive oil and a tunic for Yakeh, a pretty dress(?) for you, [12]and some scented oil for the temple of Banit. But I still haven't found [13]anyone to bring them to you.

Send me five small measures of castor oil. [14]And give some grain to Wahpre. He will be buying lumber [15]and storing it at his house. Don't get in his way—let him buy all the lumber he can find!

[16]If Reia has sold you any wool, let me know.

Greetings [17]to Tetosiri. Take good care of her! I am sending this letter to greet you.

¹⁸*Address:* To Tashai from Makkebanit son of Psami.
Let it be carried to Syene.

7. Hermopolis 6 (Cairo Univ., Arch. Mus. P. 1692)
(late sixth–early fifth century)

A

1   אל אחתי תבי מן א[חוכי בנתס]ר ברכתכי לפתח זי

2   יחוני אפיכי בש[לם ואף ... ב]רי שאל שלמכי

3   וכעת יהב מ[כבנת בר פסמי]חתנה זי נבשה כסף

4   ש׳ 6 וזוז כ[סף זוז ואזל]ואפקני אנה וברי

5   וכתבת לה ע[לה ספרה אזלי]וזבני עמר כזי תמט-

6   ה ידרכי ואו[שריהי לתשי ס]ו[ן הלו כספה זי הוה

7   בידה יהב ע[לי ל .... נבשה ומכ]בנת שאלן שלמכי

B

8   ושלם תרו מ[ן אחוכי מכבנת וכ]עת שלם בנתסר תנה

9   וברה אל ת[צפי לה וכעת הלו]אנחן בען אלף

10   ויתונה לכן לש[למכי שלחת ס]פרה זנה

11   אל אמי [תבי מן בנתסר בר] סרה אפי יבל

¹To my sister Tabi from [your brother Banitsar].
I bless you by Ptah—²may he let me see you again in good health!
My son [...] sends greetings to you.
³[Makkebanit son of Psami], Nabusha's son-in-law, paid ⁴6½ silver shekels (at the usual rate of conversion) [and got] me released—my son and I—⁵and I wrote him [a document of obligation for it. Go] buy as much wool as you can ⁶⁻⁷and send [it to Tashai at] Syene. He paid my [debt to ...] with the sum of money he had.
[Nabusha and] Makkebanit send greetings to you ⁸and Taru.
[A postscript from your brother Makkebanit:] Banitsar is well here. ⁹As for his son—don't [worry about him.] We are trying to find a boat ¹⁰to send him back on.
I am sending this letter to greet you!

¹¹*Address:* To my mother [Tabi from Banitsar son of] Sarah.
Let it be carried to Luxor.

8. Hermopolis 5 (Cairo Univ., Arch. Mus. P. 1691)
(late sixth–early fifth century)

A

אל אחתי תרו ותבי מן אחוכן נבושה ומכבנת ברכנכן   1

לפתח זי יחזני אפיכן בשלם וכעת תדען זי מדעם   2

לה מפקן לן מן סון ואף מן זי נפקת מן סון שאל   3

לה הושר לי ספר ומנדעם וכעת יהתו לן ארון   4

וביגבן והן תכלן תהיתן לן תקם יתו ביד חרוץ   5

בר ביתאלשזב זי אתה למחתה לבמרשרי אתריה   6

ומהי דה זי ספר לה הושרתן   7

B

לי ואנה נכתני חויה והות מית ולה שלחתן   8

הן חי אנה והן מת אנה לשלמכן שלחת ספרה זנה   9

אל תרו מן נבושה בר פטחנם אפי יבל   10

[1]To my sisters Taru and Tabi from your brother Nabusha (and Makkebanit). We bless you [2]by Ptah—may he let us see you again in good health!

You should know that [3]they aren't sending us anything from Syene. Sheil [4]hasn't sent me a letter or anything else since I left Syene!

They should ship us a chest [5]and a plank of . . . -wood. If you can send us some castor oil, do so by Haruz [6]son of Bethelshezeb, who is going to bring the *officials*[i] to. . . .

[7]What's wrong? Why haven't you sent me a letter? [8]Even when I nearly died of snakebite, you didn't write to see [9]whether I was alive or dead!

I am sending this letter to greet you!

[10]*Address:* To Taru from Nabusha son of Petekhnum.
Let it be carried to Luxor.

9. Hermopolis 7 (Cairo Univ., Arch. Mus. P. 1693)
(late sixth–early fifth century)

A

אל אמי עתרדמרי מן אחוכי אמי שׁ[ל]ם ו[חין שלחת לכי 1

שלם אחתי אסורי וזבבו וככי וכען עליכי מתכל אנה הוי 2

חזית על ינקיא אלכי שלם וסרז ושפנית ובניה ופטמון שלם 3

הריוטא ואחתהה לשלמכי שלחת ספרא זנה 4

B

אל אחתי עתרדי מן אֹחֹו[כי א]מׁי אפי יובל 5

[1]To my mother Atardimri from your brother Ami.

May you live [well] and long.

[2]Greetings to my sister Isiwere and Zababu and Kake. I am trusting you to look [3]after those children! Greetings to Vasaraza, and Shepeneith and her children, and Peteamun. Greetings [4]to Haryuta and her sister.

I am sending this letter to greet you!

[5]*Address:* To my sister Atardi from your brother Ami. Let it be carried to Luxor.

To a Son on a Journey

10. Padua 1 (Museo Civico di Padova)
(provenance unknown, ca. 475–450)

A

[שלם ב]ית יהו ביב אל ברי שלמם [מ]ן אחוך אושע שלם ושררת 1
[הושרת לך]

[וכעת] מן יום זי אזלת בארדחא זך לבבי לא טיב אף אמך כעת 2
ברך אנת [ליהו אלהא]

[זי יח]ו[ני אנפיך בשלם כעת מן יום זי נפקתם מן מצרין פרס לא 3
י]היב לן תנה]

[וכזי] קבלן לפחותא על פרסכן תנה במגדל כן אמיר לן לאמר 4
על זנה [אנתם קבלן]

5 [קדם] ספריא ויתיהב לכן כעת כזי תאתון מצרין
על [.....................]

6 [..פ]רסכן זי כלי כלה כעת איך ביתא עביד ואיך נפקת הן
יהו[..........]

7 [...ש]לם ומחבל לא איתי גבר הוי אל תתאשד עד תאתה
[................]

B

8 [.....................]

9 [כזי כתבת] באגרתא זילך על כתון ולבש כתונך ולבשך עבידן
[..........]

10 [....] לאמך עבדת אל תמלי לבת בזי לא איתית המו מנפי כזי
ת[אתה תמה]

11 [איתי] המו קדמתך כעת זבנת לי אנה כֹתן 1 זי כתן כעת
[............]

12 [...]כן ולבש עד תאתה שלם אמך וינקיא כלא כעת תנה הוין
[.........]

13 [ב...] למחר כתבת אגרתא זא כזי כן שמיע לן לאמר תתפטרן
[.........]

14 אל אחי שלמם בר אֹ[ו]שע אחוך אושע בר פט[.......]

[1]Greetings to the temple of YHW in Elephantine!
To my son Shelomam from your brother Oshea.

I send you greetings and wishes for your good health.

[2]Since you left on your trip, my mind has not been at ease. Neither has your mother's. I pray that [the God YHW] will bless you [3]and let me [see] you again in good health.

Since you left Lower Egypt, we have not been [paid] your salary [here]. [4]When we complained about your salary to the government officials here in Migdol, they told us, "[You should complain] about this [5][to] the bookkeepers, and it will be paid to you." So when you come back to Lower Egypt, [*you will be able to receive*] [6]your salary that was withheld.

How is the household doing, and how was your departure? If [...] will be [...] [7][...] well, and no damage was done. Be a man! Don't cry(?) until you come [...]. [8][...].

[9][You wrote] in your letter about a tunic and a garment. They have been made. [...]. [10][...] I have made for your mother. Don't be angry that

I haven't brought them to Memphis. When you [come there, [11]I will bring] them to you.

I have bought myself a linen tunic, [...]. [12][...] and a garment until you come.

Your mother and all the children are fine. We are [...] here. [13][On the ...] of Mehir I wrote this letter[k] when we got word that you would be released [...].

[14]*Address:* To my brother Shelomam son of Oshea from your brother Oshea son of Pet[...].

A Son to His Mother

11. Padua 2 (Museo Civico di Padova) (provenance unknown, ca. 425–400 B.C.E.)

A

אל אמ[ן] יהוישמע ברך שלום [שלם ושררת שניא הושרת]	1
לך שלם גלגל תנה שלם ינקיה ו[כ]ע[ת] זך [........]	2
זילי הבה לפחנום בר נבודלה ויעב[ד...............	3
יגרוהי והן איתי כסף הבי עלוהי [...........לשלמכין	4
שלחת ספרה זנה שלם ^אמי^ מנחמת שלם [..........שלם]	5
יהוישמע	6

B

[אל אמ]י יהוישמע בר[ת............]	7

[1]To my mother Yahuyishma from your son Shallum.
[I send] you greetings and best wishes for your good health.
   [2]Galgul is well here. Greetings to the children.
   That [...] [3]of mine, give it to Pakhnum son of Nabudelah so he can make [...]. [...] [4]they will sue him. If there is any money, give it to him. [...].
   [5]I am writing to [greet you]. Greetings to my mother Menahemet, [to ... and to] [6]Yahuyishma.

[7]*Address:* [To] my [mother] Yahuyishma daughter of [...].

Grain Shipments

11a. Berlin Papyrus 23000
(ca. 425–375 B.C.E.)

A

אל אחי חורי ופטמחו אׄחוכם ספנתדת שלם אחי אלהׄיא כׄלׄ|א 1
ישאלו בכל עדן וכעת

איתי לי אלף חדׄה בידכם ביני ובין מריה חזו חלקא זׄילי זי 2
יאמר לכם ארמׄנ|ׄתׄידת

למטען בה וזי צבי יעבׄדׄ לה אף חלקי באנׄר אלפא |זׄך זילׄן| הבׄו 3
על ידה איתי כסף

ש' 8 יהׄבׄת ל[.] למנתן בעבור למׄובל לביתי ואיתי כסף כרש 4
1 זי אנה יהבת

לך למזבנה |עׄבׄ|ור ליתמא כל כסף / כרש 1 ש' 8 הׄן| זבנתון המו 5
עבור ויבלתון

על בתין טׄוׄבׄ וׄהׄ|ן לא כספא הבׄו ליד ארׄ|מׄתׄיׄדׄרׄת הׄן| יהׄיׄתה עלין 6
והן עבוׄ|רׄא [..]

קים בידכׄם| הׄוׄ|דׄעו לארמתידת עלוהי |וׄהׄ|בׄוהי לׄ|ה ויזׄ|בׄנהי 7
פטמחו י |[.....]

B

עמך |בׄאׄ|לׄ|פׄא| אל ירחק מנכם עד ימטא |עׄ|לׄי 8

אל אחי חורי בר כׄמׄן ופטמחו אׄחוכם ספנתדת בר פרורתפת 9

[1]To my brothers Hori and Petemahu from your brother Spentadata.
May all the gods seek your welfare at all times.

[2]You are in possession of a boat owned jointly by me and its master.[l]
See that whatever Armatidata[m] tells you is my share [3]is loaded; do whatever he wants! And turn over to him my share of the profit for [our] shipment.[n]

There are [4]eight silver shekels I gave to [...][o] to buy grain to ship to my storehouse. And there is one silver *karsh* that I gave [5]you to buy grain for Yatma. (The total amount of the silver is one *karsh*, eight shekels.)

If you have already bought grain with them and have shipped it [6]to our storehouses, well and good. If not, give the money to Ar[mati]data; he will bring the grain to us.[p] And if [7]you still have the grain, let Armatidata know about it and give it to him so he can sell it.

[*Keep*] Petemahu [8]with you on the boat. Don't let him leave you until he arrives back here!

[9]*Address:* To my brothers Hori son of Kamen and Petemahu, from your brother Spentadata son of Fravartipata.

Notes

[a] "With you" at the beginning of no. 11a:8 is singular. The singular "(to) you" at the beginning of line 5 confirms that Hori was the more responsible member of the pair of sailors.

[b] The religious life of this community has been extensively studied. The classic study is that of Vincent 1937. See also Porten 1968 and my briefer comments in Lindenberger 2001: 153–54 and n. 51.

[c] The Aramaic is unclear. I understand the literal sense to be, "Do not buy (anything) with the garment, or release it!"

[d] For the translation, see Grelot 1972: 158 and note e.

[e] Or "frayed, ripped." See Grelot 1972: 160a; Gibson 1975: 138.

[f] The sentence is very difficult. If *'trtn* is a form of the verb *ytr* "to have in abundance," the literal sense may be something like, "If I could see what you have in abundance, I would exchange it" (cf. Porten and Yardeni 1986: 10). For other possibilities, see Grelot 1972: 160–61 note b.

[g] Or "pot." The same word, with a slightly different spelling, appears in no. 6.

[h] An alternative reading yields, "I have invested it at interest with Banitsar."

[i] Literally, "six silver shekels and a *zuz,* at one silver *zuz* (to the ten)." See the glossary (*karsh*) on this expression.

[j] Literally, "Assyrians"(?). The meaning of the Aramaic word is uncertain, but it is possibly found again in no. 18. The name of the place to which they are to be delivered cannot be identified.

[k] Or, "[. . .] tomorrow. I wrote this letter. . . . "

[l] Literally, "a boat (that is) between me and its master." The "master" is apparently Armatidata. As co-owner, he had the authority to give orders to the Egyptian sailors. Whether the term implies that he also served as captain is uncertain.

[m] The name is spelled "Armantidata" here, but "Armatidata" in line 7. Only the second form can be explained from a Persian etymology; the form with *n* is apparently a scribal lapse (Naveh and Shaked 1971: 380). In line 6, the form without *n* should be restored and will just fit the lacuna, with *t* written broadly as in line 7 (contra Porten and Yardeni 1986: 48–49).

[n] More literally, "the *'gr* for [our] ship." The word *'gr* is sometimes translated "hire, rent," but here apparently means "profit," a sense well attested in later Jewish Aramaic (see Sokoloff 1990: 35a).

[o] "To you" would fit the context, but not the visible traces of the lost letters.

[p] Or ,"he will arrange to have it sent to us." Literally, "he will bring it to us." It seems clear from context that "it" refers to the grain, not the money (Grelot 1972: 504 note k).

III

Ostraca from Elephantine

ALL BUT ONE OF THE letters in this chapter were found at the beginning of the twentieth century C.E. on the island of Elephantine in Upper Egypt. The exception, no. 17, was found at Aswan (ancient Syene), on the east bank of the Nile facing Elephantine. All of them date to around 475 B.C.E. In fact, though various senders are identified by name, the letters appear to have been written by the same hand, probably a self-employed public scribe or a moonlighting government employee (Naveh 1970: 37–38; cf. Wente 1990: 8–9). Persons in Syene wishing to send a message to family or business associates on the island had only to go to the scribe and dictate their message. A short communication would be written on an ostracon and put into the hands of the next boatman crossing over to the island, where it would be passed on to the addressee.

These letters show few of the formal marks of proper epistolary style (see the introduction, section V). They are often cryptic. Friends and relatives who have seen one another only a few hours or a few days previously have no need to explain matters of common knowledge.

These letters do not speak of great events that would attract the interest of the political or military historian, but they provide glimpses into the everyday life of the residents of this small and close-knit community. For the general historical background of these letters, see the introduction to chapter 2 above.

The subject matter is varied: an ominous dream (no. 12), the payment of debts including one owed to a religious organization (no. 13), livestock (nos. 15 and 17), foodstuffs, clothing, and other common commodities. A cryptic but intriguing note (no. 21) refers to a garment left in the temple of YHH, possibly for sacral use.

A longer and quite difficult letter (no. 18) deals with slaves. It is directed to an unnamed woman; some of the imperative verb forms are feminine. The first half relates to a complex transaction in which a female slave-artisan, a weaver, is being leased by her owner to two other persons in succession, one of whom is the writer. The note continues with a warning concerning a slave mark on one Tetosiri. This appears to refer to a second slave, though it may be an awkward reference to the same one. The details of the warning are also not clear, but it seems to be an injunction against falsifying the mark of ownership tattooed or branded on Tetosiri's arm. The second part concerns salary payments and the transport of three additional slaves.

Two letters allude to Jewish religious observances. The writer of no. 20 urges his correspondent to get down to the docks early the next day to receive a shipment of vegetables, so they can be unloaded before the Sabbath begins. In no. 19, a friend or relative of a Jewish family living on the island asks casually, "Let me know when you will be celebrating Passover." Clearly Passover was already being observed at Elephantine half a century before the so-called "Passover papyrus" (no. 30; 419 B.C.E.). Whether the writer's request reflects a time when Passover had no fixed date or whether other factors lie behind it (a delay because of ritual impurity or a possible intercalary month) cannot be determined.

Reference has already been made to the fact that there were some anomalous features of the religion of the Elephantine community (see the introduction to ch. 2, on no. 10). A possible example of this occurs in no. 27a, in which the writer greets a correspondent who is apparently Jewish, to judge by his name Haggai, with an epistolary blessing in the name of four Babylonian gods. But it is far from clear that the writer himself is Jewish. His name, Yarhu, is more likely Canaanite, deriving from the name of the moon god. If this is so, the greeting is not relevant to understanding Haggai's religion.

A Dream and Family Matters

12. Berlin, St. Mus. 1137
(ca. 475 B.C.E.)

A

1   כען הלו חלם

2   חזית ומן

3   עדנא הו אנה

4   חמם שגא

5   תחזי יח-

מליה 6

שלמ^י^ 7

B

כען הן צבתי 8

אל תזבני / המו 9

יאכלו ינקיא 10

הלו לא 11

שאר 12

קטין 13

[1]I have had a dream, [2]and since [3]then I have been [4]very feverish. [5-6]See Yahmolyah and [7]pay him![a]

[8]If you wish, [9]do not sell them.[b] [10]Let the babies eat! [11]There isn't anything [12]left, not even [13]a little bit![c]

Money for a Religious Society

13. O. Cairo 35468a
(ca. 475 B.C.E.)

על חגי אמרת 1

לאשין על כסף 2

מרזחא כן אמר 3

לי לם לאיתו 4

כען אנתננה 5

לחגי או 6

יגדל דבר 7

עלוהי 8

וינתנהי 9

לכם 10

[1]To Haggai:

[2]I talked to [3]Ashina about the money [4]for the *marzeah* society. He told [5]me [i.e., Ito], [6]"I will give it to [7]Haggai or to Yigdal." So go see [8]him [9]and get him to give it [10]to you!

A Report of Imprisonment

14. O. Clermont-Ganneau 44
(ca. 475 B.C.E.)

A

1   שלם ידניה כען לו
2   [במ]סגרא שימת ופקיד
3   [אמר לם י]כלאו מנה לחם ומין
4   [........] לי אחוטב להן
5   [............]יֺוֺם שבה

B

6   כען הן לא שֺבו לנתן תמה
7   ינפק אלי ואהך אנרס [....]
8   עֺא אף הושרו לי לֺ[.....]
9   ואכתבֺ [............]
10   וֺאֺלֺ [......]

[1]Greetings, Yedanyah!

[2]She has been put in jail, and orders [3]have been given that she is not to be provided with bread or water.

[4][...] Ahutab has [...] to me, except [5][...] the Sabbath day.

[6]If Natan has not been taken captive there, [7]let him come over to where I am, so I can go grind [meal(?)]. [8]Also send me [...], [9]and I will write [...]. [10]Do not(?) [...].

Sheepshearing

15. Berlin, St. Mus. 11383
(ca. 475 B.C.E.)

A

1   שלם אוריה כען
2   הלו תאתא זילך

רבתא מטאת למנז 3

עמרא זילה קדמא 4

מתמרט בכבא כען 5

אתא וגזה ביום 6

זי תרחֹֿמֹֿנה‎ᵈ 7

תנזנה 8

B

והן לא תנפק 9

יומא זנה שלח 10

לי וארחעה עד 11

תנפק 12a

[1]Greetings, Uriyah!

[2]Your big ewe [3-4]is ready now for shearing. The one you sent over before [5]is being combed now. [6-8]You can come shear her whenever you please. [9]If you aren't going to come [10]today, let [11]me know and I will wash her before [12a]you come over.

Bread and Flour

16. Berlin, St. Mus. 11383
(ca. 475 B.C.E.)

שלם אחטב 12b

כען על לחמא זנה 13

אכל עד מחר 14

[ע]רובה א׳ / קמח 15

שאר תנה 16

[12b]Greetings, Ahutab!

[13]About this bread—[14]eat it[e] by tomorrow [15](Friday).[f] There is still an *ardab* of flour [16]left here.

Sheep Marketing

17. Cambridge 131–133
(Aswan, ca. 475 B.C.E.)

A

|אׄלׄ אמי קוייליה ברכׄוׄ....שׄלם| 1

שלחת לכי כענת הלו הו[ד]עתכין 2

נפנא רעיא ˻קן˼ זי סחמרי בעל 3

טבתכם אתה סון עם קנה 4

לזבנה אזלי קומי 5

עמה בסון יומא 6

זנה הן תעבדן 7

B

|לה טׄ[ו]בׄה בסון יעבד לי 8

|אׄף הׄ[ו] הלו גׄזׄר לי לם אזל 9

|לבׄיׄתי וינתנו לׄ[וכׄיׄן ענז 1 עד 10

תמטאנך כען חזרו ו[....] 11

למעבד לה הלו [מׄ]ׄנׄ[יׄ]ׄן המו 12

אׄף לחם אף קמח הוׄ[13

|אתׄ[ה] ושאׄלׄהׄי 14

לם מה תבעׄי 15

[1]To my mother Qawwileyah from your son [...].

[2]I send you greetings!

This is to let you know that [3]your partner Nefna, the shepherd from Sahmeri, [4]has come to Syene with sheep [5]to sell. Come over [6-7]to Syene today to help him. If you will do [8][him a favor][h] in Syene, then he will do one for me. [9]He *promised*[i] me, "Come [10]to my house, and they will give you a goat for you[j] before [11]she arrives where you are."

They went back and [*were not able*][k] [12]to do it. They are *taking inventory*[l] of [13]bread and flour. But now [14]he has come. You ask him, [15]"What do you want us to do?"

Money and Slaves

18. Bodleian Aram. Inscr. 1 (Lost)[m]
(ca. 475 B.C.E.)

A

כענת חזו חנתא זי יהב לי אוריה לנסכא   1

הביה לגמריה בר אחיו ויערכה מן   2

שכרא ובלוה לאוריא אף חזי תטוסרי   3

זילן יכתבוה על דרעה עלא מן כתבתא   4

זۡי על דרעה הלו כן שלח לאמר זי   5

לא ישכחן עלימתה   6

מ>ת<כתבה על   7

שמה   8

B

כענת [......] [° ° ° ° ° ° ° °] הזדהרי   9

למۡלۡכיۡהۡ ולۡי למכתבה אף כזי   10

תשמעין לאמר אۡשۡריۡא יהבן פרס   11

בסון שלחۡי עלי חזי נחת קפירא   12

זי היתת ביۡ[ד]ۡי הושרוהי לי וۡקפרא זי   13

הושרת לכם מן [מۡפۡי]ۡ / נהרא   14

וۡקפירא רבא זי יהב   15

ליۡן] מלכיה הושרי   16

המו לי   17

[1]See to the *slave-girl*[n] Uriyah gave me for the weaving. [2]Give her to Gemaryah son of Ahyo and let him determine [3]her wages[o] and send her back[p] to Uriyah.

Also, see to our own Tetosiri.[q] [4]Have her marked on the arm above the mark [5]that is already there. He has written me that [6]he had better not find his servant-girl [7]marked with [8]his name.[r]

[9]Now [. . .]. Be careful that [10]Malkiyah's name and mine are inscribed.[s]

Also, when [11]you hear that the *officials*[t] are making salary payments [12]at Syene, let me know.

See to Nakht, the *slave*[u] [13]I brought along with me—have him sent to me. The *slave* [14]I sent to you from *Memphis* by river, [15-17]and the big *slave* Malkiyah gave me—have them sent to me.

Family Messages: Passover

19. Bodleian Aram. Inscr. 7
(ca. 475 B.C.E.)

A

1	אל הושעיה
2	שלמך כען חזי[v]
3	על / ינקיא עד תאת-
4	ה אחטב אל תוכ-
5	ל המו על אחרנן

B

6	הן גרסו לחמהם
7	לשו לחם קב 1 עד
8	תאתה אמהם שלח
9	לי אמת תעבדן פסח-
10	א הוי שלח שלם
11	ינקא

[1]To Hoshayah: [2]Greetings!

Take care [3]of the children until [4]Ahutab gets there. Don't trust [5]anyone else with them!

[6]If the flour for your bread has been ground, [7]make up a small portion[w] of dough to last until [8]their mother gets there.

Let me know [9]when you will be celebrating Passover.

[10-11]Tell me how the baby is doing!

Repair of a Garment

20. O. Clermont-Ganneau 70
(ca. 475 B.C.E.)

A

אל מרי מיכיה עבדך 1

גדל שלם וחין שלחת 2

לך ברכתך ליהה ולחנ[ום] 3

כען שלח / לי לבשא 4

B

זי עליך ויחטנה 5

לשלמך שלחת ספרֺא 6

[1]To my lord Mikayah, from your servant [2]Gaddul.
May you live long and well! [3]I bless you by YHH and Khnum.
[4]Send me the garment [5]you have on,[x] so it can be restitched.
[6]I am writing to greet you.

Dedication of a Tunic

21. O. Cairo 49624
(ca. 475 B.C.E.)

חזו כתוני זי 1

שבקת בית [בית] 2

יהה אמרי לאריה 3

[ו]חרמה   על סלואה 4

[1]Look after the tunic [2]I left in the temple [3]of YHH. Tell Uriyah [4]it is to be dedicated.[y]

Address: To Salluah.

Handling of Produce and the Sabbath

22. O. Clermont-Ganneau 152
(ca. 475 B.C.E.)

A

1 שלם יסלח כענת הא בקלא אוש-

2 ר מחר ערקי אלפא מחר בשבה

3 למה הן יאבד חי / ליהה הן לא נפשכ[ן]

4 אלקח אל תתכלי על משלמת

5 ועל שמעיה כען החלפי לי שער^ן^

6 ובעי^z פֿרֿא חט חמו בקט כענת

7 חי / ליהה הן לא על

8 נפשכי

B

9 [...ֹ.]נה על דבר תקבח^{aa} מה זי

10 הושרת תחת חמר^{bb} להו[ו]ֹם [כֹ]ל[א]

11 הושרתה הן משלמת לא מֹצֹאֹת

12 לי אנתי מה תאמרן תחזין אנפי

13 ואחזה אפיכי

[1]Greetings, Yislah!

Look, I'm sending you the vegetables [2]tomorrow. Get there before the boat comes in—on account of the Sabbath—[3]so they won't be spoiled. I swear to God, if you don't, I'll [4]kill you! Don't trust Meshullemet [5]or Shemayah to take care of it.

Trade the barley for me. [6]Try to get a lamb[cc].... [7]I swear to God, if you don't, [8-9]you'll have to ... yourself.

As for the ... [10]you sent in exchange for the wine, I have sent it all on to them(?). [11]If Meshullemet doesn't get here,[dd] [12-13]what will you say?

May we see each another soon!

Shopping Lists and Shipping Orders

23. O. Clermont-Ganneau 16
(ca. 475 B.C.E.)

A

הושרו / לי 1

מלח קבן 2 2

דקק וחצף 3

קפתא עלוהי 4

אף חזי 5

B

אפק לי תלי 6

וכתון 1 הן 7

יערדרן ותפק 8

אחטב / עמרֹ 9

פול / פֹּל- 10

חֹ 11

[1]Send me [2]two *qabs* of salt, [3]fine and coarse grade. [4]The basket is to put it in.

[5]Also, I want you [6]to send me[ee] a pickaxe [7]and a tunic; there is [8-9]hoeing[ff] to do. Have Ahutab send over an *omer* [10-11]of cut beans.[gg]

24. O. Clermont-Ganneau 169
(ca. 475 B.C.E.)

A

[ש]לם אחוטב כען הושרי 1

לי זעיר מלח יומא זנה 2

והן מלח לאית בביתא 3

זבנו מן אלפי עבורא 4

5   זי ביב הלו

6   לאיתי לי

B

7   מלח למשם בקֹמֹח נ]..[ת

[1]Greetings, Ahutab!

Send [2]me some salt right away—today! [3]If there isn't any salt in the house, [4]then buy some from Alpay the ferryman[hh] [5]at Elephantine. [6]I don't have [7]any salt left to put in the flour [...].

25. O. Clermont-Ganneau 228
(ca. 475 B.C.E.)

A

1   מן מיכיה על א]חוטב[

2   שלמכי כענת חזי]נפיא[

3   רבתא ואף זעירתא]לקמח[

4   אל ינפי מנהם הלו

5   שנא זי לא

B

6   ]עבדו ב[הם חזי עקא זי

7   ]הושר[ת לכי ביד פמן הבהי

8   ].... [סרי אף בעי גלדא

9   ]זי [אמרת לכי הלו עליכי

10 הו אל יאבד

[1]From Mikayah to [Ahutab].

[2]Greetings to you!

See to the large [sieve] [3]and the small one [for the flour]. [4]Don't let it be sifted without them.[ii] There is [5]a lot that [6]hasn't been [...].

See to the lumber [7]I [had] Pamin [bring you]. Give it to [8][...].[jj]

Would you also ask for the skin [9]I told you about? It's charged to you,[kk] [10]so don't let anything happen to it![ll]

25a. O. Clermont-Ganneau 125?[mm]
(ca. 475 B.C.E.)

A

מן [.....שלם]	1
כע]ן אנה[.....]	2
שלח]ת לכם לם[	3
אל תהושר לי	4
לחם ולא הו	5

B

חתם הלו כל בק‖א‖]-	6
יא טמאן הא	7
לחמא זי הוש[ר]ת[‏ם‎]	8
לי אתמל ט[מא]	9
כען אל] תהושרן[	10
לי ל]חם[.....]	11

[1][Greetings to...] from [2][...]. I [3]am writing you to say, [4]Don't send me [5]any more bread unless [6]it is sealed![nn] All of the [7]containers(?) are *impure*,[oo] so [8]the bread you sent [9]me yesterday is [impure]. [10]Don't [send] [11]me [any more] b[read...].

26. O. Clermont-Ganneau 186
(ca. 475 B.C.E.)

A

יה שלמך יהה[.......]	1
צבאת ישא]ל בכל עדן כען כזי[	2
זי וחפרע בר [.......]	3
תאת]ה הושר לי[...	4
וכב]שה ומלח[....	5
ל[.......]	6

B

עד יום שבה [הושרת לך]   7

ביד משלם נונן ...[.....]   8

ביד בעדי 3 רבר[בן ...]   9

ויהבת לה י[ו]מא זנה...]   10

גזירה [......]   11

[........]   12

[1]To [...]yah: Greetings!

May YHH [2][of hosts] bless you at all times.

When [3]the [*shipment*] of Wahpre son of [4][...] arrives, send me [5][...] and a lamb(?), and some salt [6][...] [7]before the Sabbath.

[I am having] [8]Meshullam [bring you] some fish[pp] [...] [9]and [having] Baadi [bring] three big(?) [...]. [10]I am giving it to him today [...] [11]cut up(?) [...]. [12][...].

27. O. Cairo 35468b
(ca. 475 B.C.E.)

A

[......]   1

[....] ..ל.תה   2

[....] ...תה אזל אטֹר   3

[......]   4

[....]תא   5

[....]   6

B

הושר לי שערן   7

קב 1 וש<ל>ח / ליוטב   8

כסא זעירא   9

[[1–6] *Unintelligible*] [7]Send me one *qab* of barley, [8]and send Yotab[qq] [9]the little cup.

Greetings in the Names of the Gods

27a. O. Clermont-Ganneau 277
(ca. 475 b.c.e.)

אל אחי חגי אחוך 1

ירחו שלם אחי 2

בל ונבו שמש ונר- 3

גל 4

[1]To my brother Haggai, from your brother [2]Yarhu. [3-4]May Bel and Nabu, Shamash and Nergal *bless* you *always*.[r]

Miscellaneous

Each of the two sides of this ostracon bears a different letter (cf. nos. 15 and 16, also written on the same sherd). The senders of nos. 28 and 29 are different, but the recipient is the same in both cases. It is not clear whether the two letters are related.

28. BM 45035
(ca. 475 b.c.e.)

A

שלם מיכיה מן נתן בר גמריה 1

כען אתה על מחר ולא כשרן 2

הלו שכר הו לי למדד 3

כען אל תושר למאתה 4

מחר 5

[1]Greetings, Mikayah! From Natan son of Gemaryah.
[2]He is planning to come tomorrow, but they are not ready(?).[ss] [3]I am the one hired to do the measuring![tt] [4]So don't send him over [5]tomorrow!

29. BM 45035
(ca. 475 B.C.E.)

B

6   שלם מיכיה מן ידניה כענת

7   הֹלו שֹלחת לך אתמל בשֹם

8   הודויה בר זֹכֹריה לֹם

9   אתה ליומא זנה ולא

10   אתית ביד בנתי שלח

11   לי ᵘᵘ

[6]Greetings, Mikayah! From Yedanyah.

[7]I wrote you yesterday concerning [8]Hodawyah son of Zekaryah, as follows: [9]"He is coming today." But I am not [10]having *Banitay*ᵛᵛ bring him. [11]Write me!

Notes

[a] I follow Dupont-Sommer 1948a: 109–30. The widely accepted alternative, "I saw an apparition, and it said, 'Peace' or: 'All is well'" (Levine 1964: 19; Donner and Röllig 1966–69: 2:321; and Grelot 1972: 21), cannot be reconciled with the characters written on the sherd.

[b] Or "Do not buy them."

[c] Or, interpreting *qṭyn* differently, "There are no cucumbers left" (Porten and Yardeni 1999: 169).

[d] Porten and Yardeni (1999: 160) read line 7 *zy trbʿnh*, giving a sentence that can be translated idiomatically, "You should wash her on the same day you shear her."

[e] Or "we should eat it," reading *nʾkl* in line 14. There is an ill-defined mark at the beginning of the line, possibly an error by the scribe, that Porten and Yardeni (1999: 160) read as *n*.

[f] The word *ʿrwbh* in later Jewish Aramaic is a special term meaning "day of preparation" (for Sabbath, Passover, or another religious festival). In this later usage, Sabbath eve (i.e., Friday) is usually meant unless another festival is specified. This technical usage is otherwise attested only in much later texts, however, and the phrase should perhaps be translated simply, "by tomorrow evening."

[g] Porten and Yardeni (1999: 153–54) read *hb[y]*, "Give!"

[h] Following Porten and Yardeni 1999: 153 in their reading and restoration at the beginning of lines 8 and 9. Literally, "If you will do something [good for him] in Syene...."

[i] I have followed Cowley (1929) in reading *gzr*, but the first two characters are unclear. Porten and Yardeni 1999: 153 read *mḥr* "tomorrow (I have to go...)."

[j] If this difficult sentence is interpreted correctly, the first "you" refers to the writer, the second to Qawwileyah. Such abrupt grammatical shifts of person are not uncommon in ancient Near Eastern epigraphy. I have followed Porten and Yardeni's reading (1999: 153) *lky* as being graphically preferable to Cowley's *lḥnh* (1929), "a goat for Hannah," but certainty is impossible.

[k] The characters at the end of this line (after *ḥz-*) are barely legible. Porten and Yardeni's reading *ḥzẙ zy ṭbh,* "regard (that) which is a good thing" is at least possible (1999: 153–54).

[l] Or *kpnn,* "they are hungry" (Porten and Yardeni 1999: 153–54).

[m] Though generally known by its Bodleian Library reference number, the text was transferred to the Ashmolean Museum. It was stolen many years ago and never recovered, though excellent photographs exist.

Porten and Yardeni (1999: 161–62) have at a number of points offered readings superior to those in previous publications, including the first edition of this book. Note particularly *ʾp* (line 3), *zyln* (line 4), *ḥzdhry* (line 9), *tšmʿyn* (line 11), *šlḥy* (line 12), *bydy* (line 13), *nhrʾ* (line 14), *ḥmw* and *ly* (line 17), and the ordering of the two sides. In line 9, Porten and Yardeni's reading וֹאָף before הֹזֹדֹהֹרֹי may perhaps be correct, but the characters in the only existing photograph are much less distinct than Yardeni's copy indicates. Substantial differences in reading still remain, however, and their translation of the text is almost entirely different from this one.

[n] This word is obscure and the translation based on context; see line 6 in which the unambiguous *ʿlymth* ("his servant-girl") appears to be a synonym. The same consonants recur in two fragmentary ostraca, *CIS* ii 139a:2 (= *TADD* 7.40:3) and *TADD* 7.36:2. "Slave-girl" is a plausible translation in the first example but is unlikely in the second. Porten and Yardeni's translation "*gift*" in all three cases is also apparently conjectural (1999: xlvi, 162, 181, 183).

[o] This refers to a sum paid to the correspondent as middleman, or to wages paid to the slave, a normal practice elsewhere in the Persian Empire at this time (Dandamaev 1984b: 120–21).

[p] Alternatively, "her fee," to be paid to Uriyah, the owner.

[q] An alternative translation is, "Also, see to Tetosiri. Let 'ours' (that is, our name) be marked on her arm...."

[r] The referents of the pronouns in this sentence are obscure. If Tetosiri is the weaver, it may be that Uriyah is asking the writer to inscribe his (Uriyah's) name above an older slave-mark and then warns against letting Gemaryah alter that mark. But if so, it is unclear why the writer would call the slave "our own Tetosiri."

[s] Literally, "Be careful to inscribe 'belonging to Malkiyah' and 'belonging to me.'"

[t] Literally, "Assyrians(?)." The reading is uncertain, but it is perhaps a popular term for officials in the military administration. Text no. 8 may show this same usage.

[u] The word *qpyrʾ,* found three times in this text, is unexplained. "Slave" is a conjecture based on context. What appears to be the same word occurs in two other ostraca, both in contexts that are broken and obscure. Porten and Yardeni (1999: lviii, 162) translate "pot," apparently identifying the word with Akkadian *qapīru,* a container or measure of capacity. Various other meanings have been proposed; see Hoftijzer and Jongeling 1995: 1020.

[v] There is an unintelligible stroke or smear at the end of this line. Porten and Yardeni (1999: 158) read it as the number "1" and interpret it as "singly (= alone)."

^w One *qab*.

^x Or possibly "the garment you have on account."

^y Porten and Yardeni (1999: 170) read the beginning of line 4 [*w*]*yrmh*, translating "[that] *he should drop it off* at Salluah('s)." In Yardeni's hand copy, the first partly legible letter does indeed look like *y*, but on the ostracon itself, the trace is less definitive. I believe that Dupont-Sommer's reading of the letter as *ḥ* is graphically defensible and yields a more intelligible sense.

^z Initial *waw* (rather than *nun*, as I had it in the first edition) is correctly read by Porten and Yardeni (1999: 168).

^{aa} So Porten and Yardeni 1999: 168. Dupont-Sommer (1949) reads *tqbr*. Neither word is intelligible.

^{bb} Porten and Yardeni (1999: 168) read *ḥmy* (unintelligible).

^{cc} Or "some bran." The following phrase is unintelligible. For *pr' ḥt*, Porten and Yardeni (1999: 168) read *1 w'ḥt*, "(seek) 1 (= someone) and I shall...." Near the end of the line, for Dupont-Sommer's *bqṭ* (1949), they read *bql*, "legumes."

^{dd} Porten and Yardeni (1999: 168–69) read *ysph* "If Meshullement is not concerned about me."

^{ee} Literally, "See—send me...!"

^{ff} Or "Send me a plow and a tunic; there is plowing...."

^{gg} Porten and Yardeni (1999: 159) translate *'mr* as "wool" and consider lines 10–11 unintelligible.

^{hh} Or "from the grain-boats, transport-boats."

ⁱⁱ Or "See to the large [winnowing fan] and the small one [for the wheat]. Do not let it be winnowed without them."

^{jj} Several scholars restore the damaged name as Egyptian [Peṭo]siri.

^{kk} Or "It's your responsibility"; see Porten and Yardeni 1999: 157.

^{ll} Or "Don't let it go to waste!"

^{mm} On the discovery of this ostracon, concerning which there is considerable confusion in Clermont-Ganneau's notes (hence the question mark in its number), see the *editio princeps*, Lozachmeur 1990.

ⁿⁿ The sense seems to be "without packing it properly." I am not aware of any evidence for "sealing" bread for shipment in antiquity.

^{oo} *ṭm'n*. The word ordinarily refers to ritual impurity, which may be the sense here. I follow Porten and Yardeni (1999: 185) in restoring the same word in line 9. One might also consider the possibility of a nonritual connotation for the word, in which case the complaint may be that "the containers(?) are *damaged*, so now the bread is *spoiled*."

^{pp} Possibly "three fish." Porten and Yardeni (1999: 180) read the number 3 followed by another letter (*w* or *r*). But it is difficult to reconcile Yardeni's hand copy with the photograph published by Dupont-Sommer 1957: 403.

^{qq} Porten and Yardeni (1999: 186) read *wšḥlyn ṭb* at the end of line 8, translating "and good cress, (by) the small cup."

^{rr} The short, elliptical text appears to be complete. The italicized parts of the blessing are implied but not written out. All four divinities are Babylonian.

^{ss} Porten and Yardeni (1999: 171) read this word *pšrn*, "without fail," and have the same root in line 4 (third word): *tpšr*, "do not fail." But the first letter in the word (in line 2) has an upward tick (not shown in Yardeni's drawing but clearly visible

in an infrared photograph) near the upper left end of the downward-curving line. This makes *k* the preferable reading. Such a broad head for a *p* would be very unusual in this scribe's hand. But certainty is not possible; *k* usually shows a sharp angle at the upper right rather than a downward curve, as this letter has. Whether the root *pšr* can mean "fail" is another question. It does not mean that elsewhere in Aramaic, but rather "melt, dissolve, annul a charm."

[tt] "Measuring" may refer to taking inventory of supplies (as in no. 17) or possibly to surveying. A third possibility is that the word refers to tailoring clothes; see no. 20. Note that Porten and Yardeni (1999: 171) read *mḥr* ("tomorrow"), which is also possible. In favor of it is the fact that it is a common Aramaic word, occuring two other times in this ostracon.

[uu] Porten and Yardeni (1999: 171) are definitely correct in their reading of the last two words, as against my reading in the first edition, though their translation of this phrase and of the entire letter differs from the one here. (They give *lk* as an alternative possibility for the word in line 11).

[vv] Or "my daughters" (so Porten and Yardeni 1999: 171). Lines 9–11 may alternatively be translated, following the sense but not the exact wording of Porten and Yardeni, "'Come today.' But you did not come. Send me word through Banitay/my daughters."

IV

Archives of the Jewish Community at Elephantine

THE SIX PAPYRUS LETTERS in this chapter date to a twelve-year period in the last quarter of the fifth century B.C.E. Discovered at Elephantine in 1907 by archaeologists from the Berlin Museum, they belong to the archives of one man: Yedanyah bar Gemaryah, a leader of the Elephantine Jewish community. Numbers 30 and 31 are addressed to him and his associates, and no. 35 is a memorandum of a message probably delivered to him orally. Numbers 34 and 36 are his letters or preparatory drafts, and he is probably the unnamed author of no. 33. Number 32 relates to his arrest at Thebes. The letters deal with the community's social and religious life and reflect the instability that characterized Upper Egypt during the waning days of Persian control. (See the introduction to ch. 2.)

Number 30, unquestionably the most important letter in this volume for Jewish religious history, is a damaged royal order concerning religious observance. Although it has long been known as the "Passover papyrus" (Sachau 1911: 36–40), the word "Passover" does not actually occur in the extant fragments. Dated 419 B.C.E., it is addressed to Yedanyah and the other community leaders from "your brother Hananyah," a Jew who was not resident in Elephantine.

Hananyah appears to hold a senior position in the Persian administration in Egypt. He may have been a kind of "minister of state for Jewish affairs," with authority like that exercised by Ezra in Judah and the surrounding region. Whether he is to be identified with "Hanani," the brother of the biblical Nehemiah (Neh 1:2; 7:2) is a much-debated question.

Hananyah begins by stating that he is acting on the authority of Arshama, the Persian satrap of Egypt, who had in turn received his orders from the king. (See the introduction to ch. 5.) Greeting Yedanyah and his colleagues with a stereotyped blessing in the name of "the gods"—an incongruous but not unparalleled note in Jewish correspondence—Hananyah sets forth precise commands concerning the celebration of the Feast of Unleavened Bread.

Much of the text is irretrievably lost, and what remains is perplexing. Some provisions are like those found in the Torah (Pentateuch): "do not [eat] anything leavened" (Exod 12:15, 19; 13:7; Deut 16:3–4; cf. Exod 23:18; 34:25); the reference to a week of eating unleavened bread (Exod 12:15, 18–19; 13:6–7; 23:15; 34:18; Lev 23:6; Deut 16:3–4, cf. 16:8; only Exod 12 uses both the words "fourteenth" and "twenty-first," cf. Lev 23:5); the injunction against work (Exod 12:16; Lev 23:7–8; Deut 16:8); and the association of sunset with the Feast of Unleavened Bread (Exod 12:18; contrast Deut 16:6; Exod 12:6, 18; and Lev 23:5, which speak of sundown or evening in connection with Passover).

Other features do not resemble the Torah, especially the command to "bring into your chambers [...] and seal." The missing words can hardly refer to anything except leaven, but no such command is known in the Bible or in postbiblical Jewish literature. On the contrary, leaven is supposed to be *removed* from the house; it was ordinarily burned, never stored under seal. Nor is an injunction against drinking (presumably anything made from fermented grain) found in the Bible, though it is taken for granted in the Mishnah (*m. Pesaḥ.* 3:1; etc.). The exhortation to "be pure" is paralleled only in Ezra 6:20, where it refers to the priests sacrificing the Passover lamb.

The reason for sending the letter cannot have been to introduce the celebration of Passover at Elephantine, since the festival is mentioned in letters from half a century earlier (see no. 19 and other fragmentary ostraca from the same period). Was it to link Passover and Unleavened Bread (originally two separate festivals)? Was it to establish a fixed date for Unleavened Bread or a combined festival? The uncertainty about the date of Passover intimated in no. 19 gives this suggestion plausibility. Was it to bring the celebration of Passover at Elephantine into line with its celebration in Jerusalem? It is difficult to imagine the postexilic priestly establishment in Jerusalem allowing the Passover sacrifice to be offered in Egypt. The provisions of Deut 16 centralizing the Passover in "the place that YHWH your God will choose" can, however, be interpreted as applying only to Jews residing within the Israelite homeland. The closest biblical parallels to the letter occur not in Deuteronomy but in Exod 12, a chapter conventionally attributed to the Priestly source but containing components of uncertain age. One scholar suggests a more Machiavellian interpretation—that Hananyah's intent was to warn the Elephantine community of an impending visit by a government inspector, urging them to *appear* to be acting in conformity with the regulations approved in Jerusalem (Smith 1984: 231).

To avoid prejudicing the matter and to make clear the great uncertainty surrounding the interpretation of this letter, I have followed the precedent of Albert Vincent (1937: 237–38) by offering the reader two versions: the first based only on the surviving text (no. 30a), with no reconstructions except the completion of common formulas, and the second with extensive reconstructions based on biblical parallels (no. 30b, following the restorations of Porten and Yardeni 1986).

The other letters in the chapter are placed a little over a decade later and reflect the deteriorating relations among Jews and Egyptians at Elephantine. Number 31 is addressed to Yedanyah and his colleagues from Mauzyah bar Natan, another well-known leader of the community. Mauzyah has just been released from jail in Abydos, where he had been imprisoned on a spurious charge of theft. Two Egyptians, Seha and Hor, were instrumental in gaining his release and are now on their way to Elephantine. The conclusion of the letter has usually been read as a commendation of the two men. I believe, however, that it is better interpreted as a warning from Mauzyah that despite their having helped him, they are up to no good. Number 32 speaks of riots and looting at Elephantine, naming several men and women arrested there and at Thebes. Some of the names are Jewish, some Egyptian, and some of uncertain affiliation. The letter is not dated.

The four remaining letters concern the most traumatic incident in the history of the Jews of Elephantine: the razing of their temple in 410 B.C.E. Number 33 sets the stage. Written to a Persian official whose name is lost, it accuses the Egyptian priests of bribing Vidranga, the corrupt district governor, and then running riot in the Jewish quarter of the island, stopping up a well and building a wall in the middle of the fortress. The writers demand a hearing before the regional judiciary, so that blame can be apportioned. The fragmentary conclusion alludes to vandalism in the temple and requests an injunction to prevent any such incidents in the future.

Number 34 describes the actual destruction of the temple, which took place shortly afterwards. This letter is extant in two copies, with slight textual differences. "Text A," evidently a preliminary draft, is complete and has been taken as the primary basis for the translation, although the more fragmentary "Text B" is probably closer to the version actually sent. Addressed to the governor of Judah from Yedanyah on behalf of the entire community, no. 34 is a formal petition for permission to rebuild the temple and reinstitute sacrifice. Written three years after the events, it narrates in vivid detail what happened in 410. With the collusion of the local Persian authorities, Egyptian soldiers from Syene forced their way into the temple, plundered it, and burned it. Full of indignation and bitterness, the Jewish writers observe that their temple had stood for over a century, since before the time of Cambyses (529–522 B.C.E.). They go on to describe the community's liturgical response: wearing of sackcloth, fasting, abstention from sexual relations, and a vindictive curse against the hated Persian governor, Vidranga, reminiscent in tone of the conclusion to Psalm 137. The writers allude to complaints, never answered, which they sent to religious officials in Jerusalem immediately after the event. They also state that reports were sent to Samaria, to the administrative authorities Delayah and Shelemyah, sons of Nehemiah's old nemesis, Sanballat (Sin-uballit). The administrative relationship between Judah and Samaria at this time remains one of the many historical unknowns of the period. Yedanyah and his associates take care to exonerate the satrap Arshama from any complicity in the outrage.[a]

Number 35 is the reply—or rather a succinct memorandum giving the gist of the reply—perhaps taken down orally from a courier. The Judean governor Bagavahya and Delayah of Samaria grant permission for the temple to be reconstructed and its meal and incense offerings restored. Notably absent is any permission to reinstitute animal sacrifice, as the petitioners had requested. Whether this is an accommodation to Egyptian sensitivities or a desire on the part of Persian and Jewish authorities in Palestine to downgrade the importance of the Elephantine shrine is unknown.

Letter no. 36 belongs to the same sequence of events, although its relationship to no. 35 is unclear. Like no. 35, it is a rough draft or an abbreviated file copy. The unnamed addressee was probably Arshama, the satrap (see the introduction to ch. 5), for his permission to rebuild would surely have been required. Conceding the restriction against animal sacrifice, the community leaders ask for permission to rebuild, offering a "donation" (evidently a euphemism for a bribe) to encourage the recipient to decide in their favor.

Whether the temple was actually rebuilt is impossible to say. Legal documents dated after 407 describe nearby property lines with reference to the temple precincts. But the site could have been used as a reference point even if it remained in ruins. If the sanctuary was restored, it was not used for long. The last datable document from the Jewish colonists is a fragmentary letter (not included here) from 399 B.C.E. alluding to the accession of the Egyptian king Nepherites, founder of the Twenty-Ninth Dynasty (Kraeling 1953: no. 13). With the end of Persian hegemony in Egypt, the colony vanished without a trace.

Passover (?) and Unleavened Bread

30a. AP 21 (Berlin, St. Mus. P. 13464)
(419 B.C.E.)

A

1 [אל אחי י]דניה וכנותה ח[ילא] יהודיא אחוכם חננ[י]ה שלם אחי
אלהיא [ישאלו]

2 [בכל עדן] וכעת שנתא זא שנת 5 דריוהוש מלכא מן מלכא שליח
על ארש]ם...[

3 [....]יא כעת אנתם כן מנו ארב[ע....]

4 [יומן לניסן.................עב]דו ומן יום 15
עד יום 21 ל[........]

5 [................] דכין הוו ואזדהרו עבידה
א[ל תעבדו]

6 [........................]אל תשתו וכל מנדעם זי חמיר אל
[תאכלו]

B

7 [............................ב]מערב שמשא עד יום 21
לניסן[.....]

8 [............................ה]נעלו בתוניכם וחתמו בין יומיא
[אלה]

9 [........................]א[

10 [אל] אחי ידניה וכנותה חילא יהודיא אחוכם חניה ב[ר...]

[1][To my brothers,] Yedanyah and his colleagues, the Jewish [garrison], from your brother Hananyah.

May the gods bless my brothers [2][always].

This year, year five of King Darius, the king sent to Arshama [...]. [3][...]. You should count as follows: four [...]. [4][...]. And from the fifteenth day to the twenty-first day of [...]. [5][...].

Be scrupulously pure. Do not [do] any work [6][...]. Do not drink any [...] nor [eat] anything leavened. [7][... at] sunset until the twenty-first day of Nisan [...]. [8][...]. Bring into your chambers [...] and seal [...] during [these] days. [...]. [9][...].

[10]*Address:* [To] my brothers Yedanyah and his colleagues, the Jewish garrison, from your brother Hananyah son of [...].

30b. AP 21 (Restored Version)

A

1 ‏[אל אחי י]דניה וכנותה ח[ילא] יהודיא אחוכם חננ[י]ה שלם אחי
אלהיא [ישאלו]

2 ‏[בכל עדן] וכעת שנתא זא שנת 5 דריוהוש מלכא מן מלכא
שליח על ארש[ם לאמר]

3 ‏[...............................‏°..]יא כעת אנתם
כן מנו ארב[עת עשר]

4 ‏[ומן לניסן וב 14 בין שמשיא פסחא עב]דו ומן יום 15 עד יום 21
ל[ניסן חגא]

5 ‏[זי פטיריא אבדו שבעת יומן פטירן אכלו כען] דכין הוו
ואזדהרו עבידה א[ל תעבדו]

6 ‏[ביום 15 וביום 23 לניסן כל שכר]אל תשתו וכל מנדעם זי חמיר
אל [תאכלו]

B

7 ‏[ואל יתחזי בבתיכם מן יום 14 לניסן ב]מערב שמשא עד יום 21
לניס[ן במערב]

8 ‏[שמשא וכל חמיר זי איתי לכם בבתיכם ה]נעלו בתוניכם וחתמו
בין יומי[א אלה]

9 ‏[...........................‏°..]א

10 ‏[אל] אחי ידניה וכנותה חילא יהודיא אחוכם חנניה ב[ר ...]

[1][To my brothers,] Yedanyah and his colleagues, the Jewish [garrison], from your brother Hananyah.

May the gods bless my brothers [2][always].

This year, year five of King Darius, the king sent to Arshama [saying: ...]. [3][...]. You should count as follows: four[teen [4]*days of Nisan—on the fourteenth day at twilight you shall cele*]brate [*the Passover*]. And from the fifteenth day to the twenty-first day of [*Nisan,* [5]*you shall celebrate the Festival of Unleavened Bread. You shall eat unleavened bread for seven days*].

Be scrupulously pure. Do not [do] any work [6][*on the fifteenth day and on the twenty-first day of Nisan*]. Do not drink any [*fermented drink*]. Do not [eat] anything leavened, [7][*or let it be seen in your houses from the fourteenth day of Nisan at*] sunset until the twenty-first day of Nisan [*at sunset*]. [8]Bring into your chambers [*any leaven that you have in your houses*] and seal [it] up during [these] days. [9][. . .].

[10]*Address:* [To] my brothers Yedanyah and his colleagues, the Jewish garrison, from your brother Hananyah son of [. . .].

An Accusation and a Warning

31. AP 38 (Cairo P. 3435 = J. 43472)
(late fifth century B.C.E.)

A

אל מראי ידניה אוריה וכהניא זי יהו אלהא מתן בר ישביה 1
ברכיה בר[....]

עבדך מעוזיה שלם מראי אלה שמיא ישאל שגיא בכל עדן 2
ו[לרחמן הו קדם

אלה שמיא וכעת כזי וידרנג רב חילא מטא לאבוט אסרני על / 3
דבר אבן / צרף 1 זי

השכחו גניב ביד רכליא על אחרן צחא וחור עלימי ענני 4
אשתדרו עם וידרנג

וחרנופי בטלל אלה שמיא עד שזבוני כען הא אתין תמה עליכם 5
אנתם חזו עליהם

מה צבו ומלה זי צחא ̂חור ̂ יבעה מנכם אנתם קמו קבלהם כן 6
כזי מלה באישה

לא יהשכחון לכם לכם ידיע זי עלין הו עלין מן זי חנניה 7
במצרין עד כען

ומה זי תעבדון לחור לב[ואש]כם עבדן [אנ]תם חור עלים חנניה 8
אנתם זולו מן בתין

B

נכסן לקבל זי ידכם מהשכחה הבו לה לא חסרן הו לכם בזך 9
שלח אנה עליכם הו

10   אמר לי שלח אגרת קדמתי [הן]לו חסרן שני ֗א֗ שים אחדוהי
     בבית עננ‍י זי תעבדון

11   לה לא יתכסן מן עננ‍י

12   אל מראי ידניה אוריה וכהניא ויהודיא ע[בד]כם מעוזיה בר נתן

[1]To my lords Yedanyah, Uriyah and the priests of the God YHW, Mattan son of Yeshobyah, Berekyah son of [..., from] [2]your servant Mauzyah.

[May the God of heaven] bless my lords richly at all times, and may the God of heaven be merciful to you.

[3]When commander Vidranga arrived in Abydos, he had me arrested on a charge relating to a stolen rhinestone(?) that [4]was found in the hands of the merchants.[b] Anani's servants Seha and Hor stirred up such a commotion with Vidranga [5]and Hornufi (with the help of God)[c] that they eventually got me released.

Now they are coming there to you. Watch out for them! [6]What do they really want? Whatever Seha and Hor demand from you, stand up to them, so there won't be any unfortunate rumors [7]against you. You are aware that Khnum[d] has been against us from the time Hananyah was in Egypt until now.

[8]So if you help Hor, you are [hurting] yourselves. Hor is really Hananyah's man. Should you despise *your*[e] own [9]property? Give him just what he deserves;[f] it will not be your loss!

That is why I am writing to you. He [10]said to me, "Send a letter ahead of me." If any serious loss is incurred, arrest him at Anani's house. Whatever you do [11]to him will not be concealed from Anani.

[12]*Address:* To my lords Yedanyah, Uriyah and the priests, and the Jews, from your servant Mauzyah son of Natan.

Riot and Imprisonment

32. AP 56+34 (Berlin, St. Mus. P. 13456 = Cairo P. 3439 = J. 43476) (end of fifth century B.C.E.)

A

1   [אל אחי ... אחוך יסלח שלם לי תנה]אלהיא ישאלו שלמך בכל
     עדן וכעת [......]

2   [.............................]י בר יח[..].[אזל לסון ועבד]
     ליהו֯[........]

3   הא זנה שמהת גבריא ז[י אסירו ב[ן]ב ברכיא [....................]

[.........ע]הוש

4   פחנום הא זנה שמהת נשיא [....................] [.]

זי א[שתכחו בבבא]

5   בנא ואתחדו א]סירן רמי אתת הודו אסרשות אתת הושע פלול

[.....] אתת יסלח רעיא

6   תבלא ברת משלם קולא אחתה הא שמהת גבריא זי אשתכחו

בבבא בנא ואתחדו [אסירן]

7   ידניא בר גמריה הושע בר יתום הושע בר נתום חגי אחוהי אחיו

בר מכי[ה.........]

8   בתיא זי עלו בהן ביב ונכסיא זי לקחו אתבו אם על מריהם להן

דכרו למרא[יהם כספ]

9   כרשן 120 עוד טעם לא עד יהוי להן תנה שלם ביתך ובניך עד

אלהיא יחוונני אפיך בשלם]

B

10   אל]   אחי ... בר] גדול אח[ו]ך יסלח בר נתן

[1][To my brother ... from your brother Yislah.

I am well here.] May the gods bless you always. [...]

[2][...] son of [...] has gone to Syene and has made [...] for Yeho[...].

[3][... These are the names of the men] who were imprisoned at Elephantine:

> Berekyah
> Hoshea
> [... *several names are lost* [4] ...]
> Pakhnum.

These are the names of the women who were [found at the gate [5]in Thebes and taken] prisoner:[8]

> Rami wife of Hodaw
> Isireshwet wife of Hoshea
> Pallul wife of Yislah
> Reiah [...]
> [6]Tabla daughter of Meshullam
> Qawwilah, her sister.

These are the names of the men who were found at the gate in Thebes and were taken [prisoner]:

⁷Yedanyah son of Gemaryah
Hoshea son of Yatom
Hoshea son of Nattum
Haggai, his brother
Ahyo son of Mikayah

[...] ⁸the houses they broke into at Elephantine and the goods they took. I can confirm that they have returned them to their owners,^h only they mentioned to the property-owners a sum of 120 ⁹silver *karsh*.ⁱ There is no need for any further orders to be given here concerning them.

Greetings to your household and your children until the gods let me see you again in good health!

¹⁰*Address:* [To my brother ... son of] Gaddul from your brother Yislah son of Natan.

Accusation of Stopping a Well

33. AP 27 (U. of Strasbourg Library, P. Aram. 2)
(ca. 410 B.C.E.)

A

....]תננן אׄנׄחׄנׄהׄ רׄבין דגלן זי מצריא מרדו אנחנה מנטרתן לא שבקן	1
‹‹ומנדעם›› מחבל לא אשתכח לן בשנת 14 דריוהוש [מל]כא כזי מראן ארשם	2
אזל על מלכא זנה דושכרתא זי כמריא זי חנוב אלהא [עבדׄ]ו ביב בירתא	3
המונית עם וידרנג זי פרתרך תנה הוה כסף ונכסן יהבו לה איתי קצת	4
מן יודנא זׄי מלכא זׄי ביב בירתא נדשׄו ושור חד בנׄון בׄ]מנציעת בירת יב	5
וכען שורא זך בנה במנציעת בירתא איתי באר חדה זי בניה	6
בנׄ[ון בי]רתא ומין לא חסרה להשקיא חילא כזי הן הנדיז יהוון	7
בברא [זׄ]ך מיא שתין כמריא זי חנוב ברא זך סכרו הן אזד	8
יתעבד מן דיניא תיפתיא גושכיא זי ממנין במדינת תשטרס	9
יתיׄ[דעׄ] למראן לקבל זנה זי אנחנה אמרן אף פרישן אנחנה	10

B

[.........] ךְ רֹחפניא זי ביב בֹּ[ו]רתא].........[11

[.........] ן אנחנה רבין].......[12

[.......] ה לא אשתכח ל].......[13

[.........] יא להיתיה מנח]ה[.......]   14

[.........] למעבד תמה ליהו אֹ[ו]להא].......[15

[.........] מֹ].]..[בגו].[.]לה].......[16

[.......] להן אתרודן חדה].......[17

[.............] אשרנא לקחו לנפש]ה[ום].......[18

[.......] הֹן על מראן ֿטבֿ שֹגיא עש].......[19

[.......] ד אנחנה מן חילא].......[20

[.........] הן על] מראן טב יתשים]טעם ..[21

[.......] אנחנה הן על מֹ[ר]אן טב].......[22

[.......] יהֹ[ג]ננון למנדעמתא זי א].......[23

[.....] א זי לן זי נרשו ל].....[24

[Beginning missing] We [...] our officers. The Egyptian garrison troops rioted, but we did not abandon our posts [2]and were not personally injured.[j]

In the year fourteen of King Darius when our lord Arshama [3]returned to visit the court, this is the offense that the priests of Khnum committed in Fort Elephantine [4]in collusion with Vidranga, the governor here. (They gave him a bribe of money and goods.)

There is a portion [5]of the royal storehouse(?) in Fort Elephantine. They tore it down and built a wall in the middle of Fort Elephantine. [6]The wall is still standing right in the middle of the fortress.

There was a well built [7]inside the fortress, so that the garrison had no lack of drinking water. Whenever we were confined[k] inside the fortress, [8]we could drink water from that well. Those priests of Khnum stopped up the well.

If a hearing [9]on the matter of this report is held before the judges, police, and investigators appointed over the district of Tshetres, [10]the facts will become known to our lord. We are free of[l] [11][any guilt in the matter].

[...] of Fort Elephantine [...] [12][...] we [...] our officers [...]. [13][...] is not found [...] [14][...] to bring a meal-offering [...] [15][...] to do [...] there for [the God] YHW [...] [16][...] inside [...] [17][...] except a brazier(?) [...] [18][...]. They took the fittings(?) for themselves [...] [19][...].

If it please our lord, [...] greatly [...] [20][...] we of the garrison [...] [21][...] If it please our lord, let [an order] be issued [...][22][...]. We [...]. If it [please our lord ...] [23][...] they [pro]tect the things that [...] [24][...] to [...] our [...], which they tore down.[m]

Razing of Temple and Petition for Aid

34. AP 30/31 (Berlin, St. Mus. P. 13495/Cairo P. 3428 = J. 43465) (November 25, 407 B.C.E.)

["Text A" (AP 30)]

A (Recto)

1   אל מראן בגוהי פחת יהוד עבדיך ידניה וכנותה כהניא זי ביב
בירתא שלם

2   מראן אלה שמיא ישאל שגיא בכל עדן ולרחמן ישימנך קדם
דריוהוש מלכא

3   ובני ביתא יתיר מן זי כען חד אלף[a] וחין אריכן ינתן לך וחדה
ושריר הוי בכל עדן

4   כען עבדך ידניה וכנותה[b] כן אמרן בירח תמוז שנת 14 דריוהוש
מלכא כזי ארשם

5   נפק ואזל על מלכא[c] כמריא זי חנוב זי ביב בירתא ̂אלהא ̂
המונית עם וידרנג זי פרתרך[d] תנה

6   הוה לם אנורא זי יהו אלהא זי ביב בירתא יהעדו מן תמה אחר[e]
וידרנג זך

7   לחיא אגרת שלח על נפין ברה זי רב / חיל הוה בסון בירתא
לאמר אגורא זי[f] ביב

8   בירתא ינדשו אחר נפין[g] דבר מצריא עם חילא אחרן אתו
לבירת יב עם תליהם[h]

Textual notes on no. 34: variants in Text B (AP 31).

[a] The length of the lacuna in B suggests that these words were omitted.

[b] B seems to have been longer at this point.

[c] B seems to have been longer here.

[d] כסף ונכסין יהבו לוידרנג פרתרכא זי.

[e] Inserted above the line in B.

[f] B inserts יהו אלהא ביב.

[g] B inserts זך.

[h] זניהום.

9 עלו באגורא זך נדשוהי עד ארעא ועמודיא זי אבנא זי הוו תמה
תברו ̂המו̂ אף הוה תרען

10 ̂זי אבן̂ 5 בנין פסילה̂ זי אבן זי הוו באגורא זך נדשו ודשיהם
קימן וצריריהם

11 זי דששיא אלך נחש ומטלל עקהן ̂זי̂ ארז כלא זי̂ עם שירית
אשרנא ואחרן זי תמה

12 הוה כלא באשה̂ שרפו ומזרקיא זי זהבא ̂וכספ̂ ומנדעמתא זי
הוה באגורא זך כלא לקח̂ו̂

13 ולנפשהום עבדו ומן יומי̂ מלך מצרין אבהין בנו אגורא זך ביב
בירתא וכזי כנבוזי על למצר̂ין̂

14 אגורא זך בנה השכחה ואגורי אלהי מצרין כל° מגרו ואיש
מנדעם באגורא זך לא חבל

15 וכזי כזנה עביד אנחנה עם נשין ובנין שקקן לבשן הוין וצימין
ומצלין ליהו מרא שמיא

16 זי החוין̊ בוידרננ זך כלביא הנפקו כבלא̊ מן רגלוהי וכל נכסין
זי קנה אברו וכל ̂גברין

17 זי בעו̂ באיש לאגורא זך כל̊ קטילו וחזין בהום אף קדמת זנה
בעדן זי זא באיש̂תא̂

B (Verso)

18 עביד לן אגרה ̂שלחן מראן ועל̂ יהוחנן כהנא רבא וכנותה
כהניא זי בירושלם ועל אוסתן אחוה̂י̂

---

i רברבן.

j פסלה.

k אגורא זך כלא עקהן זן[ ] ארז.

l באשתא.

m וזי כספא.

n יום.

o (?) [כ]לא].

p חוינא.

q כבלוהי.

r [גבר זן]בעה.

s כלא.

t על זנה [שלחן] שלחן על מראן [א]ף על.

19 זי עננני וחרי יהודיא[u] אגרה חדה לא שלחו עלין אף מן ירח תמוז
שנת 14 דריהוש מלכא

20 וע^ד^זנה יומא אנחנה שקקן לבשן וצימין נשיא זילן כארמלה
עבידין משח לא משחין[v]

21 וחמר לא שתין אף מן זכי ועד יום[w] שנת 17 דריהוש מלכא מנחה
ולבונ[נ]ה[x] ועלוה

22 לא עבדו באגורא זך כען עבדיך ידניה וכנותה[y] ויהודיא כל[z]
בעלי יב כן אמרי^ן^[aa]

23 הן על מראן טב אתעשת על אגורא זך למבנה בזי לא שבקן לן
למבניה חזי בעלי

24 טבתך ורחמיך ^זי^ תנה במצרין אגרה מנך ישתלח עליהום על
אגורא זי יהו אלהא

25 למבניה ביב בירתא לקבל זי בנה הוה קדמין ומחתא[bb] ולבונתא
ועלותא י{{ה}}קרבון[cc]

26 על מדבחא זי יהו אלהא בשמך ונצלה עליך בכל עדן אנחנה
ונשין ובנין ויהודיא

27 כל[dd] זי תנה הן כן[ee] עבדו עד זי[ee] אגורא זך יתבנה וצדקה יהוה
לך קדם יהו אלה

28 שמיא מן גבר זי יקרב לה עלוה ודבחן[ff] דמן כדמי כסף כנכרין
1 לך ועל זהב על זנה

29 שלחן הודען אף כלא[ff] מליא באגרה[gg] חדה [hh]שלחן ^בשמן^[hh] על
דליה ושלמיה בני סנאבלט פ^ח^ת שמרין

---

[u] יהוד.

[v] משחן.

[w] זך ע[ר]נא ועד זנה יומא].

[x] B omits -ו.

[y] B appears to have had an additional phrase in the lacuna.

[z] כלא.

[aa] אמרן.

[bb] *Sic!* The word is lost in B, but would presumably have been corrected to ומנחתא.

[cc] נקרב.

[dd] כלא.

[ee] תעבד זי עד.

[ff] {{בכלא}} [lacuna] דמי כסף כנכרן אלף על. The lacuna evidently contained a text slightly longer than that of A.

[gg] אגרה.

[hh] בשמן שלחן.

30   אף בזנה [ii]זי עביד לן [^]כלא[^][ii] ארשם לא ידע ב 20 למרחשון שנת
17 דריהוש מלכא

[1]To our lord Bagavahya, governor of Judah, from your servants Yedanyah and his colleagues the priests at Fort Elephantine.

[2]May the God of heaven richly bless our lord always, and may he put you in the good graces of King Darius [3]and his household a thousand times more than now. May he grant you long life, and may you always be happy and strong!

[4]Your servant Yedanyah and his colleagues report to you as follows:

In the month of Tammuz in the fourteenth year of King Darius, when Arshama [5]left and returned to visit the court, the priests of the god Khnum in Fort Elephantine, in collusion with Vidranga,[n] the military governor here, [6]said, "Let us get rid of the temple of the God YHW in Fort Elephantine!"

Then that criminal Vidranga [7]wrote a letter to his son Nafaina, commandant at Fort Syene, as follows, "Let the temple[o] in Fort Elephantine [8]be destroyed!" So Nafaina came at the head of some Egyptian and other troops to Fort Elephantine with their pickaxes.[p]

[9]They forced their way into the temple and razed it to the ground, smashing the stone pillars there. The temple had [10–12]five[q] gateways built of hewn stone, which they wrecked. They set everything else on fire: the standing doors and their bronze pivots, the cedar roof—everything, even the rest of the fittings and other things. The gold and silver basins and anything else they could find in the temple, [13]they appropriated for themselves!

Our ancestors built that temple in Fort Elephantine back during the time of the kings of Egypt, and when Cambyses came into Egypt, [14]he found it already built. They pulled down the temples of the Egyptian gods, but no one damaged anything in that temple.

[15]After this had been done to us, we with our wives and our children put on sackcloth and fasted and prayed to YHW the lord of heaven:

[16]"Show us our revenge on that Vidranga:
May the dogs tear his guts out from between his legs!
May all the property he got perish!
May all the men [17]who plotted evil against that temple—all of them—be killed!
And may we watch them!"

[ii] B adds כלא זי עביד לן.

Some time ago, when this evil [18]was done to us, we sent letters to our lord, to Yehohanan the high priest and his colleagues the priests in Jerusalem, to Avastana, brother [19]of Anani, and to the Judean nobles. None of them ever replied to us.

From the month of Tammuz in the fourteenth year of King Darius [20]until this very day, we have continued wearing sackcloth and fasting. Our wives are made like widows. We do not anoint ourselves with oil, [21]nor do we drink wine. And from that time until this, the seventeenth year of King Darius, no meal offering, incense, or burnt offering [22]has been offered in the temple.

Now your servants Yedanyah, his colleagues, and all the Jews, citizens of Elephantine, petition you as follows:

[23]If it please our lord, let consideration be given to the rebuilding of this temple, for they are not allowing us to rebuild it. Take care of your loyal [24]clients and friends here in Egypt. Let a letter be sent to them from you concerning the temple of the God YHW, [25]allowing it to be rebuilt in Fort Elephantine just as it was formerly. If you do so, meal offerings, incense, and burnt offerings will be offered [26]in your name on the altar of the God YHW. We will pray for you constantly—we, our wives, our children, the Jews—[27]everyone here.

If this is done, so that the temple is rebuilt,[r] it will be a righteous deed on your part before YHW the God of [28]heaven, more so than if one were to offer him burnt offerings and sacrifices worth a thousand silver talents, and gold.

Thus [29]we have written to inform you. We also reported the entire matter in a letter in our name to Delayah and Shelemyah, sons of Sin-uballit (Sanballat), governor of Samaria. [30]Also, Arshama did not know anything about all these things that were done to us.

Date: The twentieth of Marheshwan, seventeenth year of King Darius.

Memorandum on Reconstructing the Temple

35. AP 32 (Berlin, St. Mus. P. 13497)
(shortly after 407 B.C.E.)

זכרן זי בגוהי ודליה אמרו   1

לי זכרן לם יהוי לך במצרין לממר ‖קד‖   2

3 קדם ארשם על בית מדבחא זי אלה ‹‹שמי››

4 שמיא זי ביב בירתא בנה

5 הוה מן קדמן קדם כנבוזי

6 זי וידרנג לחיא זך נדש

7 בשנת 14 דריוהוש מלכא

8 למבניה באתרה כזי הוה לקדמן

9 ומנחתא ולבונתא יקרבון על

10 מדבחא זך לקבל זי לקדמין

11 הוה מתעבד

[1]Memorandum: What Bagavahya and Delayah said [2]to me:

Let this be on record for you in Egypt.

[3]Official of Record: Arshama.

Concerning: The temple of the God of [4]heaven that was built at Fort Elephantine [5]long ago, before the time of Cambyses, [6]which "that criminal Vidranga" razed [7]in the fourteenth year of King Darius.

[8]Let it be rebuilt on its original site [9]and let meal offerings and incense be offered up on [10]the altar just as was formerly [11]done.

A Petition and a Bribe

36. AP 33 (Cairo P. 3430 = J. 43467)
(shortly after 407 B.C.E.)

1 עבדיך ירניה בר גמ[ריה] שמה 1

2 מעוזי בר נתן שמה [1]

3 שמעיה בר חגי שמה 1

4 הושע בר יתום שמה 1

5 הושע רב נתון שמה 1 כל גברין 5

6 סונכנן זי ביב בירתא מה[חסן]ן

7 כן אמרן הן מראן [...]

8 ואגורא זי יהו אלהא זילן יתבנה

9 ביב בירתא כזי קדמ[ן ב]נה הוה

10 וקן תור ענז מקלו [ל]א יתעבד תמה

11 להן לבונה מנחה[.........]

12 ומראן אודיס יעבד[.........]

13   נתן על בית מראן כ[......]
14   שערן ארדבן אל[ף]

[1]Your servants named below:
  Yedanyah son of Gemaryah
  [2]Mauzi son of Natan
  [3]Shemayah son of Haggai
  [4]Hoshea son of Yatom
  [5]Hoshea son of Nattun
—five men in all [6](Syenians, who hold property in Fort Elephantine)—
[7]We declare as follows:

If our lord [*will give permission*] [8]for the temple of our God YHW to be rebuilt [9]in Fort Elephantine as it was previously, [10]we agree that no sheep, ox, or goat is to be offered as a burnt offering there, [11]but only incense and meal offering [...].

[If] [12]our lord will make a ruling [on the matter], [13]we will make a donation to our lord's household of [... of silver], [14]and one thousand *ardabs* of barley.

Notes

[a] Pierre Briant has recently challenged the conventional reconstruction of the events leading up to the destruction of the temple and Vidranga's role in them. He argues that the relevant letters from the Elephantine Jewish community should be taken, not as a straightforward description of historical events, but as a partisan effort to persuade the Persian authorities to reverse a decision on the question whether the Jews had proper authorization to build their temple on a plot whose ownership was contested. For his reconstruction, see Briant 1996.

[b] The word *rkly*> means either "merchants" (perhaps referring to receivers of stolen goods) or "slanderers" (i.e., false witnesses). In either case, Mauzyah implies that the charges against him were false.

[c] Literally, "in the shadow of the God of heaven." The sense may be "under oath" or "under safe-conduct."

[d] Apparently a faction associated with the Egyptian temple of Khnum at Elephantine is meant.

[e] The text reads "*our* own property." Apparently the scribe inadvertently wrote the last letter as -*n* ("our") instead of the second-person singular possessive form -*k*. The two letters are very similar.

[f] Literally, "Whatever your hand finds, give it to him"; cf. 1 Sam 10:7.

[g] The word "gate" may refer to a law court. If so, we may translate, "who were tried at the court in Thebes and were put in prison."

[h] Or, following the restoration of Porten and Yardeni (1986: 60), "[They left] the houses they had broken into at Yeb and did indeed return to their owners the goods they had taken."

[i] The vaguely worded sentence may refer to a penalty negotiated between the householders and the defendants, or it may hint obliquely at a bribe. One hundred twenty *karsh* was an immense sum, some ten kilograms (twenty-two pounds) of silver, equivalent to nearly eight years' income for a small family (Porten 1968: 75).

[j] Or "We were not found to be at fault."

[k] Or "mobilized."

[l] Or "We are separated from."

[m] Porten and Yardeni (1986: 64) restore, "to [*build*] our [*Temp*]le which they demolished"; similarly, Grelot (1972: 405 and note u) restores "altar-house." However, the word "temple" is conjectural, and it is by no means clear that this text refers to the same events that are described in no. 34.

[n] For this phrase, B reads, "offered a bribe of silver and goods to Vidranga."

[o] B adds: "of the God YHW."

[p] B: "weapons."

[q] B adds: "great."

[r] B: "If you do (this) so that the temple may be rebuilt...."

V

Letters from Persian Officials

ALL BUT ONE OF THE letters in this chapter were acquired by the Bodleian Library at Oxford in 1943–44 and published by G. R. Driver in 1954. No details concerning their discovery are known, but it is clear from internal evidence that they were found in Egypt, possibly at Memphis or somewhere in the western Delta. They were written on leather and were found stored in a leather bag that contained between fifteen and twenty documents, some of which are now too fragmentary to be read. Twelve are included here (nos. 37–48).[a]

All twelve letters are associated with Arshama, satrap of Egypt during the last half of the fifth century. Most are from him, and the rest concern officials closely associated with him. Since the letters are undated, their sequence cannot be determined, except for the general observation that nos. 37–40 are earlier than nos. 41–48. In the latter group, Nakhthor holds the position that earlier belonged to Psamshek ("the former steward," no. 43). A thirteenth letter from Arshama's administration, written on papyrus (no. 49), was found at Elephantine. All of these letters deal with administrative concerns.

Most, perhaps all, of the letters in the group of twelve originated outside of Egypt. They were not all written from the same place. Numbers 44 and 45, taken together, place Arshama in Babylon. Yet no. 47 implies that he is *not* in Babylon, since he has to communicate with an associate there by letter. Susa, the primary seat of the Persian government, is a likely alternative (cf. nos. 33 and 46).

The letters cover several years. Driver suggests that they were sent during Arshama's prolonged absence from Egypt in 410–407, referred to in the letters of chapter 4 (nos. 33 and 34), but that is most uncertain. There must have been other such trips to transport rents, goods, and slaves and to deal with other details of administering Arshama's lands in Mesopotamia and Syria. The letters in this chapter and those in chapter 4 both speak of insurrections. Such events happened repeatedly throughout the fifth century, however, and without more information we are often unable to correlate them for dating purposes. Number 49, the one dated letter in the chapter, was written in 411 B.C.E. Nothing in it implies that Arshama was away from Egypt at the time.

A good deal is known about Arshama from Greek and ancient Near Eastern sources. Achaemenes, his predecessor as satrap of Egypt, was a brother of King Xerxes, and Arshama himself was a kinsman of the royal family. Although the Aramaic texts refer to him as "Prince Arshama," his exact relationship to the king is unknown. Appointed by Artaxerxes I in 454, in the aftermath of the rebellion of Inaros (see the introduction to chapter 2), he held office for half a century, passing from the scene just before Egypt rebelled anew at the end of the fifth century.

In the letters relating to the destruction of the Elephantine temple (chapter 4), the writers state repeatedly that Arshama was away from Egypt and had no involvement in the incident. He apparently took an extended leave in Babylonia and Persia between 410 and 407. Arshama was an exceedingly wealthy absentee master of a network of estates scattered throughout the empire. The letters in this chapter refer to his estates in Upper and Lower Egypt; cuneiform texts preserve the financial records of grazing lands belonging to him in central Babylonia; and letter no. 41 alludes to additional domains in Assyria and Syria.

Other names keep recurring in the letters. Psamshek is the steward, Egyptian overseer of Arshama's estates, apparently in both Upper and Lower Egypt (nos. 37–39; cf. no. 43 for the restoration of the title in no. 37). We meet him later in charge of a slave convoy in Babylon (no. 47). Nakhthor, the Egyptian who took over Psamshek's job as steward, performed so incompetently that he found himself forced to answer charges of mismanagement (no. 43), theft, and personal abuse of the household staff (no. 47). Other characters include the Persian Artavant (nos. 37, 39–40), never addressed by a title, but apparently Arshama's second in command, and Prince Varuvahya, a Persian absentee landlord residing in Babylon and a peer of Arshama (nos. 44–45).

Except for no. 49, the letters deal with estate management, concerns such as the appointment of stewards (nos. 37 and 42), payment of rents (nos. 44–45), and administrative complaints of various sorts. Two letters concern slaves. Number 39 authorizes punishment of a number of slaves who escaped from a transport convoy, and no. 40 demands the release of a group of slaves wrongly imprisoned during an uprising. Another (no. 38) threatens to discipline an officer who will not obey the orders of Arshama's chief steward. Estate managers had no formal authority in military matters, so far as we know, but local commanders were expected to look after the interests of the satrap.

Three letters call for more extended comment. Number 41 is a requisition for rations for a traveling party headed by Nakhthor that was bound for Egypt. Although sometimes described as a "passport," it is neither that nor an official authorization for travel rations—though such documents have been found at Persepolis (Hallock 1985: 588–91). The letter is issued on Arshama's personal authority, addressed to six of his estate managers in Mesopotamia and Syria, and authorizes supplies only while the group is passing through his domains. Vast areas outside his jurisdiction are not covered. Of course, the distinction between "official" and "personal" authority would have been blurred in the case of such a highly placed personage. The group was authorized to sojourn only one day at each place (cf. *Did.* 11:5).

For the first part of its journey the party appears to have followed the famous "Royal Road" described by Herodotus (*History* 5.52–53). This well-engineered and well-guarded highway, equipped with royal staging posts and caravansaries, ran from Susa northward and westward across the empire all the way to Sardis, some 2,500 kilometers (1,600 mi.) distant, with a connecting link to Ephesus on the Mediterranean coast. Royal mounted couriers were said to traverse it in a week; a party on foot required three months.

Nakhthor's group, perhaps starting out in Susa, would have followed this road northwest through Arrapha (modern Kirkuk). Lairu (biblical Lair, 2 Kgs 19:13) lay somewhere along the first part of the route, in northeastern Babylonia near the Elamite border. From Arrapha they would have proceeded northwest to Arbela, ancient cult city of the Assyrian goddess Ishtar, where Arshama had another estate. The Arzuhina estate was apparently in the same general region, as were possibly some of the other sites mentioned in the letter (Driver 1965: 56–59; Cogan and Tadmor 1988: 235). Following the highway northwest of Arbela, the party would have crossed the Tigris at Nineveh (near Mosul).

At that point they would have left the Royal Road. An ancient Assyrian road running westward past Guzanu (Tell Halaf) and Haran would offer a more direct route. Near Haran they could have turned south, following a secondary road down to the Euphrates highway. Then, if there existed a desert shortcut to Tadmor (Palmyra), that would have been the quickest way to Damascus. Otherwise, they would have taken the longer road through Aleppo and Hamath (Hama). From Damascus, the route is straightforward: south through Hazor and Megiddo to the coast road down to Egypt (see the map).

A second unusual letter (no. 46) contains a unique commission to one of Arshama's artisans in Egypt to prepare several sculptures or statuettes for him: two were on an equestrian theme, the others not specified. The fact that the sculptor was known in Susa suggests he was an artist of some repute among the Persian aristocracy.

Persian ruling circles had great admiration for the skill of Egyptian artisans. A century before this letter was written, Darius I (521–486) used Egyptian goldsmiths, woodworkers, and other artisans in the construction of his new palace at Susa, and Egyptian themes are widely found in Persian art. Among the Achaemenid artistic creations that can still be seen are a stylized gold statuette of a horseman (Dandamaev and Lukonin 1989: 272) and another of a chariot with a driver, a soldier, and a three-horse team. The front of the chariot depicts the Egyptian god Bes (Gershevitch 1985: pl. 44a). Egyptian motifs also appear on Persian seals (Gershevitch 1985: pl. 48ab).

The third text for special comment is no. 49, the only administrative document found at Elephantine that relates to Arshama. It concerns repairs to a boat. The most difficult letter in this collection, it is full of untranslatable shipyard jargon and technical terms, some of which are loanwords from Egyptian and Persian, and some of which are quite unknown.

The chancery scribes' habit of giving an epitome of earlier correspondence allows us to see in this letter the operation of the Achaemenid bureaucracy at its most convoluted. Four levels of previous administrative action are summarized before getting down to the business at hand (see Whitehead 1974: 124).

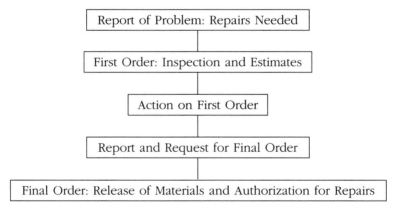

The letter is signed by "Anani the scribe, Chancellor." His identity is unknown. He has been described as a Jew who rose to the position of chancellor at Arshama's headquarters in Memphis. However, several persons named Anani are among the Jews at Elephantine, and the name is not distinctively Jewish (Stark 1971: 106; Benz 1972: 382). The letter does not specify where he is, and it is not known whether the title "chancellor" was used in more than one level of government. His office could have been at Memphis or in the regional chancery at Syene. There are no clear grounds for identifying him with the Anani mentioned in no. 31.

On arrival, these letters passed through the hands of Egyptian file clerks who left their mark. One added his name in demotic on the outside of nos. 44 and 46, and the notations on no. 49 include a longer note in demotic.

Appointment of a Steward

37. AD 2 (Bodleian Pell. Aram. XII)
(provenance unknown, written from
Babylon or Susa; late fifth century B.C.E.)

A

מֻן ארשם על אר[תונ]ת שלם ושררת שֹנוֹא הושרת לךְ וכעת 1
דשנא מן מֻלכא ומני יהב לעחחפי

עלימא זילי זי פק[יד] הוה בין בניא זילי זי ב[ע]ליתא....... 2
פסמֻשךְ ברה זי עחחפי זי כען

פֻ[ק]יד עבד חלפוהי בין בניא זילי זי בעליתא ו[ו]תח[ו]תיתא.... 3
......דֹֻש[ו]נא זכי זֻ[ו]ן מן מלכא ומני

[ו]יהב לעחחפי פסמשׁךְ ברה שליט יהוי למנשא דשנא זכי תמה 4
במ[צ]רין

B

[מֻ]ן ארשם ברביתֻ[א] על [ארתונת..........] 5
על דשנא 6
זי עֹֻחֹחֹפֹי 7
פֹֻקֹידֹא זֹֻי 8
[.....] 9

[1]From Arshama to [Artavant]

I send you greetings and best wishes for your good health.

[2]Concerning: The [grant] given by the king and by me to my man Ahhapi, who has been steward of my various estates in [Upper and Lower Egypt].

Ahhapi's son Psamshek, who has now [3]been given his father's position as steward of my various estates in Upper [and] Low[er Egypt, has requested] that the grant given to Ahhapi by the king and by me [4]be transferred to him.

His son Psamshek is hereby authorized to receive said grant there in Egypt.

[5]*Address:* From Prince Arshama to [Artavant in Egypt].
[6]*Docket:* Concerning the grant [7]of Ahhapi [8]the steward who [9][. . .].

Reprimand to an Insubordinate Officer

38. AD 4 (Bodleian Pell. Aram. II)
(provenance unknown, written from
Babylon or Susa; late fifth century B.C.E.)

A

מן ארשם על ארמפי וכעת פסמשך / פקידא זילי שלח עלי כן   1
אמר ארמפי עם חילא זי לידה לא משתמען לי

בצבות מראי זי אמר אנה להם כעת ארשם כן אמ[ר] צבות ביתא   2
זילי זי פסמשך יאמר לך ולחילא זי לידך זכי

אשתמעו לה ועבדו כן י[ד]יע יהוה לך הן פסמשך א[ח]ר קבלת   3
מנך ישלח עלי חסן תשתאל ונסת פתגם

יתעבד לך בנסרו ידע טעמא זנה אחפפי ספרא   4

B

מן [א]ר[ש]ם על ארמפי   5
על זי פסמש[ך]   6
אמר לא משתמ[ען]   7
לי   8

[1]From Arshama to Armapiya.
My steward Psamshek has informed me as follows:

> Armapiya and the troops under his command are refusing to obey [2]the orders I have given them concerning my lord's affairs.

Now I, Arshama, declare:

In any matter concerning my household about which Psamshek gives orders to you or the troops under your command, [3]you are to obey those orders to the letter! You have been warned. If Psamshek sends me another complaint about you, you will be called strictly to account and will be severely disciplined.

[4]Bagasrava has been informed of this order.

Ahpepi
Scribe

[5]*Address:* From Arshama to Armapiya
[6]*Docket:* Concerning Psamshek's [7]report of insubordination.

Slaves

39. AD 3 (Bodleian Pell. Aram. VII + Frag. 7.1)
(provenance unknown, written from
Babylon or Susa; late fifth century B.C.E.)

A

1   מן ארשם על ארתונת שלם ושררת שניא הושרת לך וֹ[כעת
   פסֹ[מֹשך שמה בר עחחפ[ין עלימא זילי קבל

2   בזנה כן אמר כזי אנה הוֹיֹת אתה [עֹ[ל [מֹראֹי.....עבֹ[דֹן זי עחחפי
   אבי זי אנה מ[......................]ׄׄׄ[

3   אחרי על מראי פסמשכחסי שמה [בר .... 1 .... בר ....[טרי 1
   עחחפי בר פ[..]ׄ.[בתחף 1 אהרֹ[...]

4   בר פסמשך 1 פשובסתי בר חור[......]חפמו 1 פסמשך בר
   וחפרעמחי 1 [.....]יֹ בר וח[....1]

5   כל גברן 8 נכסי לקחו וקרקו מני כען הן על מראי טב ישתלח
   על ארתונֹת[כזי עבדיא]אֹלכי

6   אהקרב קֹדמוהי סרושיתא זי אנה אשים / להם טעם יתעבד /
   להם כעת ארשם[כן אמר פסֹ[מֹ[שׄכחסי]

7   זכי וכנותה עבדי עחחפי זי [פסֹ[מֹשֹך יהקרב קדמיך [תֹמה] אנת
   שם טעם סרושֹ[יתֹ[אׄ זי פסמשך [ושים]

8   להם טעם למעבד זכי יתעבד / להם

B

9   מן ארשם בר / [בֹיתא על ארתונת זי במצֹ[וֹרין

[1]From Arshama to Artavant:

I send you greetings and best wishes for your good health.

My man Psamshek son of Ahhapi has registered a [2]complaint here as follows:

> While I was on the way to see my lord [...] slaves of my father Ahhapi, whom I [...] [3]after me to my lord—
>> Psamshekhasi son of [...]
>> [...] son of [...]
>> Ahhapi son of [...][b]
>> [...] [4]son of Psamshek
>> Pashubasti son of Hor
>> [...] son of [Sha]hpemu
>> Psamshek son of Wahpremahi
>> [...] son of Wah[pre]
> [5](eight persons in all)
> —took my property and ran away from me.
> Now, if it please my lord, let word be sent to Artavant [that the slaves] [6]I am sending him should be punished as I have ordered.

Now I, Arshama, declare:

In the matter of this Psamshekhasi [7]and his companions, slaves of Ahhapi whom Psamshek is sending to you there—you are to give orders that the punishment demanded by Psamshek [8]should be carried out.

[9]*Address:* From [Prince] Arshama [to Artavant] in Egypt.

40. AD 5 (Bodleian Pell. Aram. IV)
(provenance unknown, written from
Babylon or Susa; late fifth century B.C.E.)

A

מן ארשם על אֹרתהנת שלם ושררת שגיא הושרת [לֹך] וכעת   1
בזנה קדמי שלם

אף תמה קדמוֹיֹך] שֹלם יהוי וכעת איתי גברן חיל[כֹין] עבדן זילי   2
במצרין

פרי[מֹ]אֹ שמה 1 אמוֹן שמה 1 סרך שמה 1 תענדי [שֹ]מֹה 1 ....] [מֹי   3
שמה 1 סדסבנז שֹמֹ[מֹ]ה [1]

אֹ[..]ֹם שמה 1 סרמנז שמה 1 כא שמה 1 בנפרן שמה 1 פיתרענז   4
שמה 1 אסמרוף

5   שמה 1 מוסרם שמה 1 כל גברן 13 אבשוכן ממנין הֿוֿוֿ בין בניא
זילי זי

6   בעליתא ותחתיתא אחר כזי מצרין מרדת וחילאֿ הנדיז הוו אדין

7   פרֿיֿמא זך וכנותה לא שנציו למנעל / בבירתא אחר [..י]נֿחֿרו
לחיא אחד המו

8   עמה הוו כען הן עליך כות טב מנך יתשם טעם כזי איש
מנדעם באיש לא

9   יעבד לפירמא זך וכנותה ישתבקו עבידתא זילי יעברו כזי
קדמן

B

10   מן [אֿ]רשם בר / ביתא על ארתהנֿתֿ זי בֿ[מצרי]ן

11   עֿלֿ חיֿלכיא

12   [....]זיֿלֿיֿ

13   [שֿ]נֿציו.[

14   [..] למֿהוֿה

[1]From Arshama to Artahant.[c]
I send you greetings and best wishes for your good health.

All is well with me here; [2]may it also be well with you there.

There are certain Cilician slaves of mine in Egypt [3]whose names are
listed as follows:

>   Pariyama
>   Ammuwana
>   Saraka
>   [. . .]
>   [. . .]miya
>   Sadasbinazi
>   [4][. . .]
>   Sarmanazi
>   Ka
>   Bagafarna
>   Piyatarunazi
>   [5]Asmaraupa
>   Muwasarma

(thirteen persons in all, pressers[?] who were appointed in my various
estates in [6]Upper and Lower Egypt).

When the Egyptians rebelled and the garrison had to be mobilized, [7]this Pariyama and his co-workers were unable to get into the

fortress. Later, that criminal *Yenḥaru* arrested them [8]and has kept them in custody.

Now, if you concur, let an order be issued that no one is to harm [9]Pariyama and his co-workers. They should be released and go back to work for me.

[10]*Address:* From Prince Arshama to Artahant in [Egypt].
[11]*Docket:* Concerning the Cilicians [12][...] my [13][...] were unable [14][...] to be [...].

Rations for a Traveling Party

41. AD 6 (Bodleian Pell. Aram. VII)
(provenance unknown, written from
Babylon or Susa; late fifth century B.C.E.)

מן ארשם על מרדך פקי[ד]א זי ב[א.][כד נבודל[נ]ן פק[ו]דא] זי   1
בלער זתוהי פקידא [זי בא]רזוחן אפסתבר פ[קי]ד[א] זי בארבל
[חל.] ומתלבש בנפרן פקידא

[ז]י בסעלם פרדפרן והו.][.ת [פ]ק[י]די[א] זי בדמשק [וכע]ת [ה]א   2
נחתחור שמה פקידא זי[ל]י אזל מצרין אנת[ם] הבו [לה פ]תף מן
ביתא זילי זי במדינתכם

יום ליום קמח חורי חפנן תרת[ו]ן קמח רמי חפנן תלת חמר או   3
שכר חפנן תרתין [...]ר חד ולעלימוהי גב[ר]ן עשרה לחד ליומא

קמח חפן חדה עמיר לקבל רכשה והבו פתף לגברן חלכין תדרין   4
אמן חד כל תלתה עלימן זילי זי אזלן עמה מצרין לגבר

לנבר ליומא קמח חפן חדה פתפא זנה הבו להם מן פקיר על   5
פקיד לקבל אדרנא זי מן מדינה עד מדינה עד ימטא מצרין

והן יהוה באתר חד יתיר מן יום חד אחר זי יומיא אלך יתיר   6
פתף אל תנתנו להם בנסרו ידע טעמא זנה רשת ספרא

[1]From Arshama to:
    Marduk, official in [...]
    Nabu-delani, official in Lairu,
    Zatuvahya, official in Arzuhina,
    Upastabara, official in Arbela, [...], and Lubash
    Bagafarna, official [2]in Saalam,
    Fradafarna and [...], officials in Damascus:

This is to introduce my official, Nakhthor by name. He is on his way to Egypt. You are to issue him daily provisions from my estates in your respective provinces as follows:

[3]White flour: 2 cups
Fine[d] flour: 3 cups
Wine or beer: 2 cups
[...]: 1

For his retinue (ten men in all), for each one daily: [4]Flour: one cup, plus sufficient fodder for his horses.

You are also to issue provisions to two Cilicians and one artisan (three in all), my servants, who are accompanying him to Egypt: [5]Flour: one cup daily per man.

Issue these provisions, each official in turn, along the route from province to province, until he arrives in Egypt. [6]If he stops in any place more than one day, do not give them any extra provisions for the additional days.

Bagasrava has been informed of this order.

Rashta
Scribe

Restoration of an Estate to Its Rightful Heir

42. AD 8 (Bodleian Pell. Aram. XIII)
(provenance unknown, written from
Babylon or Susa; late fifth century B.C.E.)

A

מן ארשם על נחתחור כנזסרם וכנותה וכעת פטוסרי שמה ורשבר 1
עלים [ז]י[ו]לי שלח עלי כן אמר איתי פמון ש[מ]ה א[ב]י כזי

יוזא במצרין הוה זך אבד ובנה זי הוה מהחסן פמון שמה אבי 2
בית זרע א′ 30 זך א[ו]שתבק בגו בזי נשי ביתן כלא [א]בדו........]

לי בנה זי פמון אבי יתעשת / לי ינתנו / לי אהחסן כעת ארש[ם] 3
כן / אמר הן כ[נ]נ[ם] הו כמליא אלה זי פטסרי שלח [עלי זי פמון]

[ש]מה אבוהי זך כזי יוזא הוה במצרין אבד עם נשי [ביתה וב]ג[נ]ה 4
זי פמון ז[ך] א[ב]והי בית זרע א′ 30 זך אשתב[ק........]

לא עביד לעלים אחרן זילי מני לא יהיב אחר אנה בנה זי פמון 5
זך יהבת לפטסורי אנתם החווהי יהחס[ן] והלכא

לקבל זי קדמן פמון אבוהי הוה חשל יחשל על ביתא זילי   6
ארתוהי ידע טעמא זנה רשת ספרא

B

מן ארשם על נחתחור פקידא̊ ‏[כנזסֺ]רם וכנותה ‏[המרכ]ריא זי   7
במצרין

[1]From Arshama to Nakhthor, Kenzasirma, and his associates.

One of my tenant farmers,[e] Petosiri by name, has sent me word as follows:

Concerning my father Pamun—[2]he perished [during] the uprising in Egypt.

The estate my father Pamun held, a thirty-*ardab* plantation, was abandoned at that time, because all our household staff perished. [3]The estate of my father Pamun [was not given] to me.

I appeal to you. Let it be given to me to hold.

Now I, Arshama, declare:
If Petosiri has reported to [me] accurately,
— that this Pamun, [4]his father, perished along with [his household] staff,
— that the estate of that Pamun, his father, a thirty-*ardab* plantation, was abandon[ed, ... and]
— [5]that it was not made over [to my own estate,] or given by me to any other servant of mine,

then I give the estate of said Pamun to Petosiri.

You are to notify him. He will hold it [6]and will pay the land-tax to my estate just as his father Pamun did formerly.

Artavahya has been informed of this order.

Rashta
Scribe

[7]*Address:* From Arshama to Nakhthor the steward, Kenzasirma, and his associates the accountants in Egypt.

Reprimand to a Negligent Steward

43. AD 7 (Bodleian Pell. Aram. I)
(provenance unknown, written from
Babylon or Susa; late fifth century B.C.E.)

A

1　מן ארשׁם על נחתחור וכעת קדמן כזי מצריא מרדו אדין
<פ>סמשך פקידא / קדמיא גרדא ונכסיא

2　זילנא [זין] במצרין חסין נטר כן כזי מנדעם כסנתו לא הוה מן
ביתא זילי אף מן אתר אחרן גרד

3　אמנן וספזן ונכ[סן א]חרן שפיק בעה ועבד על ביתא זילי וכען
תנה כן שמיע לי כזי פקידיא זי

4　[בתח]תיתא בשוזיא מתנצחן גרדא ונכ[סין מר]א[י]הם חסין נטרן אף
אחרנן בעין מ[ן] אתר אחרן

5　ומהוס[פן ע]ל בית מראיהם ואנתם [כ]ן לא עבדן כען אף קדמן
שלחת עליכם על / ז[נ]ה אנתם [א]תנצחו / גרדא

6　ונכ[ס]יא זילי[ן] חסין טרו כן כזי מ[נד]עם כסנתו לא יהוה [מ]ן ביתא
זילי אף / מן אתר א[ח]רן גרד אמנן

7　[ו]ספזן שפיק בעו והנעלו בתרבצא זילי וסטרו בשנתא זילי
ועבדו על ביתא זילי כן כזי פקידיא

8　[קד]מיא הוו עבדן כן ידיע יהוי לך הן / מן / גרדא או / מן
נכסיא אחרנן זילי מנדעם כסנתו יהוה

9　ומן א[תר] אחרן לא תבעון ולא תהוספון על / ביתא זילי / חסין
תשתאלון ונסת פתגם יתעבד

10　לך [אר]תחי ידע טעמא זנה רשת ספרא

B

11　מ[ן] ארשם על נחתחור פקידא זי במצרין בתחתיתא

12　[על] הנדר[זא]

13　זי [.....]

[1]From Arshama to Nakhthor:
　During the recent Egyptian uprising, Psamshek, the former steward,
went to great pains to guard our domestic staff and property [2]in Egypt, so

that my estate suffered no loss whatever. He even sought out additional staff from elsewhere, [3]artisans of all kinds, and property, and appropriated them for my estate.

Word has reached me here that the other stewards of [4]Lower Egypt have been active during the recent outbreaks, going to great pains to guard their masters' personnel and property, seeking out others from elsewhere, and [5]adding them to their masters' households. But you[f] have not been doing this.

I have written to you about this before. You are to care diligently for my staff [6]and property so that my estate shall suffer no loss whatever. And you are to seek out additional staff from elsewhere, [7]artisans of all kinds, and attach them to my service. Mark them with my mark, and put them to work in my estate, just as [8]your predecessors used to do.

Know this: if any loss whatever to my staff or other property is incurred [9]and you do not seek out replacements from elsewhere and add them to my household, you will be held strictly accountable and will be severely punished.

[10]Artahaya has been informed of this order.

Rashta,
Scribe

[11]*Address:* From Arshama to Nakhthor, steward in Lower Egypt.
[12]*Docket:* Concerning the instructions [13]that [. . .].

Overdue Rent

44. AD 10 (Bodleian Pell. Aram. IX)
(provenance unknown, written from
Babylon or Susa; late fifth century B.C.E.)

A

1   מן ארשם / על נחתחור כנזסרם וכנותה וכעת ורׄוהי בר ביתא
    בזנה כן אמר לי בנא לם זי מן מראי יהיב / לי

2   במצרין זך מנדעם מן תמה לא מהיתין עלי הן על מראׄי לם כות
    טב אגרת מן מראי תשתלח על נחתׄחׄוׄר פקידא

3   והמרכריא כזי הנדרז יעבדון לחתובסתי שמה פקידא זילי זי
    עד מנדת בגיא אלך יהנפק ויהיתה עלי עם מנדתא זי

4   מהיתה נחתׄחׄוׄר כעת ארשם כן אמר אנתם הנדרז עבדו
    לחתובסתי פקיד ורוהי זי עד מנדת בגיא זי ורוהי אספרן

והראבנו יהנפק ויהיתה ויאתה עם גנזא זי מני שים להיתיה   5
בבאל ארתוהי ידע טעמא זנה רשת ספרא

B

מן ארשם על נחתחור פקידא |כֿנזֿ|סרם וכנותה המרכר|וֿ|א זי   6
במצרין

על הנדרזא   7

[......] זי   8

[........]   9

[........]   10

<demotic>   11

[1]From Arshama to Nakhthor, Kenzasirma, and his associates.
Prince Varuvahya has reported to me as follows:

> Concerning: The estate given to me by my lord [2]in Egypt.

> Nothing has been brought to me from there. If it please my lord, let a letter be sent to Nakhthor the steward [3]and the accountants to the effect that they should instruct my steward Hatubasti to release the rent for those estates and send it to me along with the rent that [4]Nakhthor is bringing.

Now I, Arshama, declare:

You are to instruct Hatubasti, Varuvahya's steward, to release the rent of Varuvahya's estates—full payment [5]with interest—and to bring it when you come, along with the revenues I ordered brought to Babylon.

Artavahya has been informed of this order.

Rashta
Scribe

[6]*Address:* From Arshama to Nakhthor the steward, Kenzasirma, and his associates the accountants.
[7]*Docket:* Concerning the instruction [8]that [9–10][. . .].
[11]*Demotic notation:* Hotephep.

45. AD 11 (Bodleian Pell. Aram. V)
(provenance unknown, written from
Babylon; late fifth century B.C.E.)

A

מן ורוהי על נחתחור וכנדסירם וכנותה וכע[ת] תנה אנה קבלת 1
לארשם על אחתבסתי

פקידא זילי זי מ[נ]ד[ת]א] מנדעם לא מהיתה לי אח[ר .....]ת 2
מהיתין [בבאל כע[ת] אנתם

אתנצח[ו]ן] והנדרזא עבדו לפקיד[א] זי[לי עד מנדת [בניא אלך 3
יהי[תה עלי בבאל כן עב[דו]ן]

כזי לי תחדרן אף ה[א] שנ[ן] ש[ג]יא זי בנא ז[ך .....] לא כשר אף 4
אחתבסתי פקידא [זילי]ן

או אחוהי או ברה יאתה עלי בבאל עם מנדתא 5

B

מן ור[ו]ה[י על נח[ת]ח[ו]ר] וחנ[ו]רסירם] פ[ק. [.............] 6

[1]From Varuvahya to Nakhthor, Kendasirma, and his associates:

I have registered a complaint here to Arshama concerning my steward Ahatubasti, [2]that he is not bringing me any of the [rent]. [...] is being brought to [Babylon].

Now you [3]are to give my steward strict instructions to bring the rent [of those estates] to me in Babylon. Do it [4]to please me! As you know, [the finances of] that estate have not been in order[8] for many years.

Furthermore, [my] steward Ahatubasti [5]or his brother or his son is to come to me in Babylon with the rent.

[6]*Address:* From Varuvahya to Nakhthor, Hendasirma [*sic*] [....]

Commission for a Sculptor

46. AD 9 (Bodleian Pell. Aram. III)
(provenance unknown, written from
Babylon or Susa; late fifth century B.C.E.)

A

מן ארשם על נחתחור כנזסרם וכנותה וכעת חנזנ֯נ֯י שמה   1

פתכרכר עלי֯ןמ֯א֯ן זילי זי בנסרו היתי שושן זך פתפא הב

לה כאחרנ֯ן ֯ולנשי ֯ביתה֯ / נרד בדיכרן ֯ז֯֯ן֯לי ויעבד פתכרן זי   2

פרש [....] יהו֯ו֯ן ו֯֯י֯ע֯ב֯ד פתכר סוסה עם רכבה לקבל זי קדמן

עבד קד֯ן֯מ֯י

ופתכרן אחרנן והושרו יהיתו עלי א֯פריע לעבק ול֯עבן֯ק ארתוהי   3

ידע טעמ֯א זנ֯ה רשת ספרא

B

מן ארשם / על / נחתחור / פקי֯ן֯דא כנ֯ז֯ס֯ר֯ם֯ ו֯כ֯נ֯ו֯ת֯ה   4

המ֯ו֯ר֯כ֯ו֯ר֯יא זי במצרין

[..ע֯ל֯]   5

[....]   6

[....]   7

[....]   8

<demotic>   9

[1]From Arshama to Nakhthor, Kenzasirma, and his associates.

Concerning: Hinzanay,[h] a sculptor and a servant of mine, whom Bagasrava brought to Susa.

Issue rations [2]to him and his household, the same as those given to the other artisans[i] on my staff.

He is to make statues of a horseman [...]. They should be [...]. And he is to make a statue of a horse with its rider, just as he did previously for me, [3]and other statues. Have them sent to me just as soon as you can! Artavahya has been informed of this order.

Rashta
Scribe

[4]*Address:* From Arshama to Nakhthor the steward, Kenzasirma, and his associates the accountants in Egypt.

[5–8][*Fragments of four illegible short lines*]

[9]*Demotic:* Hotephep.

Complaints

47. AD 12 (Bodleian Pell. Aram. XIV)
(provenance unknown, written from
Babylon or Susa; late fifth century B.C.E.)

A

1   מן ורפש על נחתחור וכעת מספת [פּ]קידא זי לי ^שלח עלי^ כן /
אמר בבל לם אגרת מן ארשם יהבת֯

2   על [פּסמשׁ]ך בר עחחפי למנתן חלכין [גברן 5֯] ובבל [....] לי
חלכין 5 כל גברן [10]

3   אחר חלכיא גברן 5 שאל מן [נחתּ]חור ולא יֹהֹב / לי כעת ורֹפש
[כֹ]ן אמר הא אנת

4   חזי אגרת ארשם זי היתיו / על פֹּסמשׁך על חלכיא / זי מלכו /
לי גברן 5 [....] הב למספת

5   חלכ[ו]א אלך 5 שטר / מן זי יהבו בבבאל גברן 5 אף / קבילה
שלח עליך חמרא לם

6   זי בפֿפֿרם ועבור ארקתא כלא נחתחוֹר לקח / עבד לנפשה כעת
חמרא עבורא ומנד[עֹם]

7   אחרן זי לקחת כלא התב / הב למספת יעבד על ביתא זילי
למה כזי תאתה בזנה

8   מה זי לקחת זיני תשלם ותשתאל על / זנה אף מספת שלח גרדא
לם זי מראתי

9   כתש ונכסן לקח / מנה כעת אנת וגרדא זילי עבידה לא אית לך
ומה זי

B[†]

לקחת [נ]כֹסֹן מֹן / גרדא התב הב / להם　10

כו[ן] כזי מספת קבילה תובא לא ישלח　11

עֹ[ליך]　12

C

מֹן ורפש עֹל [נח]תחור פקידא זי ב[מ]צרֹ[י]ן　13

על [....]　14

זי [.....]　15

מספת [....]　16

[.........]　17

---

[1]From Varfish to Nakhthor:
My steward Masapata has sent me word as follows:

> A letter from Arshama was delivered [2]to Psamshek son of Ahhapi in Babylon instructing him to give me five Cilician men. He gave me five additional Cilicians in Babylon—[ten] men in all.
> [3]Later, Nakhthor was asked for the other five Cilician men, but he did not give them to me.

Now I, Varfish, declare:

You [4]are to follow the instructions in the letter of Arshama that was delivered to Psamshek concerning the five Cilician men. [You are to] give Masapata [5]those five Cilicians over and above the five men given to him in Babylon.

On another matter, he has sent me a complaint against you:

> Nakhthor has misappropriated the [6]Papremis[j] wine and all the field grain.[k]

The wine, the grain, and anything [7]else you took—give it all back to Masapata. He is to transfer them back to my estate. Otherwise, when you come here, [8]you will pay damages for what you took and will be punished for this.

[†]Written sideways along the right margin.

On still another matter, Masapata has send word:

> He has beaten up my lady's household staff [9]and has taken property from her.

You are to have nothing whatever to do with my household staff.[1] And as for [10]the property you took from the staff, give it back to them, [11]so that Masapata doesn't have to send another complaint [12][against you].

[13]*Address:* From Varfish to Nakhthor [the steward in] Egypt.
[14]*Docket:* Concerning [...] [15]which [...] [16]Masapata [17][...].

Complaint of Unsatisfactory Goods

48. AD 13 (Bodleian Pell. Aram. X)
(provenance unknown, written from
Babylon or Susa; late fifth century B.C.E.)

A

1 מן אר]תו]חן[ין] על נחתחור שלם ושררת שגיא הושרת לך וכען]ת
אנ]ת אתנצח].....[

2].....[כן]ן עבד כזי לאלהיא ולארשם תחן]ד'ין אף זי הושרתْ].....[
עלי ביד אנאْ].......[

3].....[תחדו כתן / 1 גْלדי תולע 2 זך היתי עלי להן לא].....[
אנת הושרת וْ].....[

4]..........[סרת ואנה ל]א[ן חדית אנת שגיא פתן]ס]תו לי
ומנ]...[תْמ].[

5].......[אלהיא שלם ישמו לך

B

6 מן ארתחי על נחתחור

[1]From Artahaya to Nakhthor:

I send you greetings and best wishes for your good health.

You should be careful [...]. [2]Do this so that you may please the gods and Arshama.

Now the shipment you sent [has been delivered] to me by Ana[-....]
[3][...] a tunic, and two purple skins were delivered to me, but [I am] not [satisfied with them]. You have shipped [me things I don't need,] [4][...] and I am not pleased.

You have always given me excellent service[m] and [...]. [5][...]. May the gods grant you good health!

[6]*Address:* From Artahaya to Nakhthor.

A Boatyard Work Order

49. AP 26 (Cairo P. 3432 = J. 43469)
(Elephantine; January 11, 411 B.C.E.)

A

מן ארשם על וחפרעמחי וכעת בלא]........................[1

עלין מתרדת נופתא לם כן אמר פסמסני]ת ....[2

כרכיא כן אמרו ספינתא זי מהחסנן אנֹחֹנה עדן הוה אופשרה 3
למע]בד ....[

יתנגד על]תֹ[בלא וישתלח על המרכריא זי גנזא המו עם 4
פרמנכר]יא ....[

יחו ואופכרתה יעבדו וישתלח על מן זי הוה אשרנא הנדונה 5
ואחרן זי]......[

ינתנו ולעבק אופשרה יתעבד ואחרן זי מני שליח עליהם על 6
זנה שלחו וכן]אמרו.......על[

חלא זי לקבל בו]ֹרתא ב].....[ה מֹתֹרֹדֹת נופתא החוין ספינתא 7
נחוי זי ביד פסמסנית].......[

כל תרין נופתֹ^יֹ^א זי כרכיא נגידה על תבלא ואנחנה החוין 8
לשמשלך וכנותה פרמנכריא שמו ב]ר[

כנופי סנן נגריא ספיתכן וכן אמרו עדן הוה אופֹשֹ]רֹ[ה למעבד 9
זנה אשרנא זי אפיתי אופשרה

למעבד עקי ארז ואר חדתן טף אמן עשרה שים]ל[בטק אמן 10
תמנין בפשכן תלתה בגו סגנן אמן עשרה

ותרין שף עשרה וחמשה חד]ל[אמן עשרן סעבל אמן שבען 11
חנן לבטנא תלתה קלעס לקֹומתא חד

12 עקי חלא אמן שתן פחטמוני לפערער חד לאמן תרין אפסי תחת
    חלא חמשה מסמרי נחש ופרזל

13 מאתין עקי ארז לובר חסין תמיס אמן עשרן כלא יהיתה
    חליפתהם לובר ותבירן על גנזא עזלי

14 כתן עבין כרשן מאה ותמנין רקען כרשן מאתין וחמשן עקי ארז
    חדתן חנן תרין לחד אמן חמשה

15 פשכן תלתה בפשכן תלתה לחלא מסמרי נחש מאה וחמשן לחד
    פשכן תלתה מאתין שבען וחמשה

16 לחד צבען עשרה כל מסמרין ארבע מאה עשרן וחמשה טסן זי
    נחש אמן עשרן מסמריהם מאתין

B

17 עקי ארז לובר דשות מצן כנכר חד מנן עשרה כלא הוספה
    כברי כרשן עשרה ולהנדרונה זרניך כרשן מאה

18 ויהוספון על עקיא זי יתיהב על טף בארכא לחד פשכן תלתה
    חפוש ועל פתיא ועביא צבען תרין ועל

19 שים בארכא לחד פשכן תלתה חפוש ועל פתיא צבען תרין
    ועל שף וחניא בארכא לחד פשך חד ועל

20 סעבל עקי חלא דרי תמיס בארכא לחד פשכן תלתה חפוש
    ועל פתיא צבע חד עזלי כתנא רקעתא

21 זרניכא כבריתא במתקלת פרס יתיהב לם אשרנא זנה
    יתיהב עֹל / יד שמו בר כנופי סגן

22 נגריא ספיתכן לעינין אופשר ספינתא זך ולעבק יעבד כזי שים
    טעם כעת ארשם כן אמר אנת עבד

23 לקבל זנה זי המרכריא אמרן כזי שים טעם עננ ספרא בעל
    טעם נבועקב כתב

24 וחפרעמחי [....] יתיהבֹ לתובֹה בֹל [..ל ....] כותה
    [........]

25 כזי שים טעם [....]ל[כתב

26 <demotic>

27 מן ארשם זי במצ[ר]ין על וחפרעמחי [.............]

28 נבועקב ספרא ב 13 [ל]טבת שנת 12 דריו[הוש מלכא]

[1]From Arshama to Wahpremahi.

Bel-[...[n] the ... and ... the ... have sent me word as follows: ...] [2]to us. Mithradata the boatman has sent us word as follows:

Psamsineith [son of ... and ... son of ..., the two] [3]Carian [boatmen], have reported to me: "It is time to make repairs[o] on the boat we hold."[p] [We sent word to Arshama, and he said to us as follows:]

[4]Let it be brought into dry dock, and let word be sent to the treasury accountants. They and the estimators(?) [...] [5]are to be shown [the boat], and should make an estimate(?). Let word be sent to whomever is in charge that [6]they should supply [whatever] materials, paint, etc., [are required] and that the repairs, etc., ordered by me should be made immediately.

They sent back word [as follows:

We had it drawn up on] [7]the sand opposite the fortress [...], and Mithradata the boatman showed the boat to us. We report that it was brought into dry dock by Psamsineith and [...], [8]the two Carian boatmen. We showed it to Shamash-shillek and his associates the estimators(?) and Shamaw son of [9]Kanufi the master boatwright(?), and they said as follows: "It is time to make repairs(?)."

Following is a list of materials needed(?) for repairs(?).

[10]New Cedar and ... -wood:

... <*tp*>[†]	10 cubits
... <*sym*> for ...	80 cubits by 3 handbreadths
(including ...'s	12 cubits)
[11]... <*šp*>'s	15, each 20 cubits long
... <*s'bl*>-wood	70 cubits
... <*ḥnn*>'s for the hold	3
... for the mast[q]	1

[12]Wood for the Gunwale:

Mooring-post for the prow(?)	1, two cubits long
Stanchions(?) under the gunwale	5

Bronze and Iron Nails:	[13]200

Strong Well-Seasoned(?) Cedar:

Panelling	20 cubits

[†] A sign such as <*tp*> indicates consonants of untranslatable words.

Note: For all of the above, he should bring the old(?) and broken materials being replaced to the treasury.

[14]Canvas: 180 *karsh* by weight

Metal Plating(?):   250 *karsh*

New Cedar:
  . . .'s   2, each 5 cubits long, [15]3 x 3
                                           handbreadths

Bronze Nails for the Gunwale: 150, 3 handbreadths each
                                           275, [16]10 fingerbreadths each
                                                Total nails: 425

Bronze Plating: 20 cubits + 200 nails for it

[17]Well-Seasoned(?) . . . -Cedar:
  . . .   1 talent, 1 *mina*

Miscellaneous:
  Sulfur   10 *karsh*
  Arsenic for paint   100 *karsh*

[18]To be added to the lumber for delivery:
  Onto the . . . <*tp*>:   length, 3 handbreadths overcut(?)
                                           width and thickness, 2 finger-
                                           breadths

  Onto the [19]. . . <*šym*>:   length, 3 handbreadths overcut(?)
                                           width, 2 fingerbreadths

  Onto each . . . <*šp*>
     and . . . <*ḥnn*>:   length, 1 handbreadth

  Onto the [20]. . . <*sʿbl*>, the
  wood for the gunwale(?)
  and the panel sections, (to
  each of the above):   length, 3 handbreadths overcut(?)
                                           width, 1 fingerbreadth

Note: The canvas, the plating, [21]the arsenic, and the sulphur should be given according to the Persian weight.[r]

Send word: These materials are to be handed over to Shamaw son of Kanufi, chief [22]carpenter and master boatwright(?), so the boat can be repaired immediately, as ordered.

Now I, Arshama, declare: Follow [23]the instructions of the accountants, as ordered!

Anani the scribe,
Chancellor

Nabuaqab wrote it

[24]*Additional notations:* Wahpremahi [...] to be given [...] accordingly [...] [25]as ordered. [...] wrote. [26]<Demotic>: Sasobek wrote [...] The boat [...].

[27]*Address:* From Arshama in Egypt [to Wahpremahi].
[28]*Scribe and date:* Nabuaqab, scribe, thirteenth of Tebeth, twelfth year of [King] Darius.

Notes

[a] Fairly extensive restorations of additional fragments of these letters have been made by Porten and Yardeni 1986, 1999.

[b] Porten and Yardeni (1999: 135, 150) restore the damaged Egyptian name as P[*shenpe*]berekhef.

[c] A variant or misspelling of the Persian name "Artavant."

[d] For this translation, see Hinz 1973: 40.

[e] Evidently a Persian loanword meaning "food-warden" (Hinz 1973: 42). The person in question is administrator of a tenant farm.

[f] Though the letter is addressed to a single administrator, the pronouns here are plural.

[g] Or "that estate has not produced its proper [rent] for many years."

[h] The reading and derivation of the name are uncertain.

[i] Or "stonecutters" (Grelot 1972: 318c).

[j] The word has been identified with "Papremis" (a Delta town whose exact location is unknown) mentioned in Herodotus, *History* 2.59, 63, 71, 165 (Grelot 1972: 74c). It may refer to a variety of wine or simply to the place where it was stored.

[k] Possibly "seed grain."

[l] Literally, "Now you and my household staff—there is no business!"

[m] The literal sense seems to be, "You are very *praiseworthy* [a Persian loanword of uncertain meaning] to me," but the writer appears to contrast former good service with the present complaint.

[n] Perhaps "Bel-iddin" or another common Akkadian name of the period.

[o] Or "to make a . . . for the boat we hold." The meaning of the key word, apparently a Persian loan, is not known.

[p] The term refers to property held in tenure and is commonly used of lands.

^q Or "bow."

^r The Egyptian and Persian systems of weights did not exactly correspond. See *karsh* in the glossary.

VI

Two Hebrew Petitions and a Royal Order

DURING THE PAST HALF-CENTURY, two remarkably similar Hebrew petitions from the time of the Judean monarchy have come to light. Both apparently date from the second half of the seventh century B.C.E., locating them within a few years of the time of the reforming king Josiah (640–609). In each, a person of fairly low social position (a laborer in one case, a widow in the other) appeals to a person in authority.

The first of these (no. 50) was discovered in 1960 by Israeli archaeologists excavating a small Iron Age fortress near Yavneh-Yam between Jaffa and Ashdod (the site has since been named Mezad Hashavyahu). It is a palm-sized ostracon composed in reasonably good classical Hebrew. Whether or not it was written by a trained scribe is a matter of some debate. Most of the characters are written legibly and clearly, though the fourteen lines of script meander somewhat clumsily and the style is rather awkward and repetitive.

The petitioner at whose dictation the letter was written—it is doubtful he wrote it himself—is a poor farm laborer, perhaps a corvée worker doing forced labor on state-owned lands (Yeivin 1962: 8–10; Pardee 1982: 24). The addressee is an unnamed person in a position of authority. The Hebrew word translated "governor"[a] in both petitions is a rather unspecific term, unless qualified by other words, and can be used of various kinds of civil and military authorities.

The laborer claims that his outer garment has been unjustly appropriated by a certain Hoshayahu. Israel's oldest legal traditions forbid a creditor to take a garment in pledge and keep it overnight (Exod 22:25–26 [Eng. 22:26–27]). In Deuteronomy, the same prohibition is followed by an injunction "not to oppress the hired servant who is poor and needy" (Deut 24:12–15; cf. v. 17). Amos refers to a breach of this ancient commandment in listing the sins of the Israelites of his day (Amos 2:8). Although Hoshayahu's offense was not precisely the same as the act forbidden in

Exodus, since there is no suggestion in the letter that the garment was taken in pledge for a loan, it is clear that his action was contrary to the spirit of Torah and prophets alike. The document allows a fleeting glimpse of rural Israel toward the end of the monarchy: a poor laborer, harvesters laboring in the heat of the day, an oppressive foreman, an ancient custom flouted, a humble appeal to the nearest person with the power to redress the wrong.

The second petition (no. 50a), also an ostracon, has been known only since the 1990s. It belongs to a private collection, and its original provenance is unknown. On the basis of the paleography, it appears to have been written around the same time as no. 50. The Hebrew style is also very similar, though the neat script looks more like the work of a trained hand. The petitioner in this case is a woman whose husband had recently died childless. She appeals to the "governor" that she be granted the right to his estate. (The word translated "estate" is the same word used in Numbers and Joshua for the allotments of land given to the various tribes [see especially Josh 13–19] and of the entire land as the "inheritance" of Israel in Deuteronomy.)

At several points the text is ambiguous, and the notes with the translation indicate alternative possibilities. I am following the interpretation of the editors of the *editio princeps* in assuming that Amasyahu, mentioned in lines 5–6, is the name of the deceased husband and that he apparently discussed the disposition of his estate with the governor before his death, a fact of which the widow now reminds the official (see Bordreuil, Israel, and Pardee 1996: 74–76; 1998: 10–12). She asks that the governor "grant" her the land (literally "give it into her hand"), perhaps implying not outright ownership but the use of the land for her lifetime. In the final sentence, the widow refers to another field already given to the brother of the dead man, who as the closest male relative might have laid claim to the entire inheritance, probably meant as a hint that he already has his share and that justice demands that she receive hers.

The similarity in the structure and language of the two appeals is striking. Clearly this was a genre with a well-established pattern that could be adjusted according to the case (numbers in the outline below indicate lines in the two inscriptions):

	No. 50	No. 50a
Blessing	—	1
Address to the official	1–2a	2
Statement of the precipitating circumstances	2b–9	3a
Availability of corroborating testimony (and declaration of innocence)	10–12a	—

Appeal for action	12b–15	3b–6a
Note on attendant circumstances	—	6b–8

The third text in this chapter (no. 50b) is roughly contemporaneous with no. 50a, and like 50a, its provenance has not been identified. It belongs to the same modern collection as 50a and appears to have been written by the same scribe (Bordreuil, Israel, and Pardee 1998: 3). In content it is unique: a royal command from "King Ashyahu" concerning the donation of a quantity of silver, to be delivered to an official of the Jerusalem temple named Zechariah.

Despite its great intrinsic importance, this letter also raises perplexing questions. The name Ashyahu (or "Eshyahu") is found elsewhere in the Hebrew letters (no. 59; partially restored also in 51:11) and is well-attested in other Hebrew inscriptions and seals (Avigad and Sass 1997; Gogel 1998: 297). But no king of this name is known in the Hebrew Bible. A number of biblical kings are known by alternative names, however, such as Jehoiachin/Coniah (in several different Hebrew spellings). The most likely identification of Ashyahu is Josiah, during whose reign there is said to have been a high temple official named Zechariah (Zekaryahu; 2 Chr 35:8).[b] The letter, with its curt command from the king concerning the temple donation, also raises questions about the relative authority of king and priest at this time in looking after the temple. In Kings and Chronicles, they are depicted virtually as coequals. The letter, along with other evidence from the ancient Near East, suggests otherwise (Sérandour 1998: 6).

A few scholars raised doubts about the authenticity of nos. 50a and 50b shortly after they were published (Eph‘al and Naveh 1998).[c] Early laboratory tests appeared to confirm their authenticity (Rollston 1998), but Rollston now states that he has become convinced the ostraca are forged, after all.[d] Nevertheless, the arguments against their authenticity published so far are less than compelling, and I am treating them here—albeit with caution—as genuine.[e]

A Judicial Petition

50. Mezad Hashavyahu Ostracon (IM 60–67)
(near Yavneh-Yam; second half of seventh century B.C.E.)

1 ישמע אדני . השר

2 את דבר עבדה . עבדך

3 קצר . היה . עבדך . בח-

4 צר / אסם . ויקצר עבדך

5 ‏ויכל ואסם כימם . לפני שב-

6 ‏ת כאשר כל [ע]בדך את קצר וא-

7 ‏סם כימם ויבא . הושעיהו בן שב-

8 ‏י . ויקח . את בגד עבדך כאשר כלת

9 ‏את קצרי זה ימם לקח את בגד עבדך

10 ‏וכל אחי . יענו לי . הקצרם אתי בחם

11 ‏הֹשֹמֹש אחי . יענו לי . אמן נקתי . מא-

12 ‏[שם השב נא את] בגדי ואם לא . לשר להש-

13 ‏[ב את בגד עֹבֹדֹרך ותתֹן] אלו . רח-

14 ‏[מם והֹשֹ]בֹת אֹת [בגד ע]בדך ולא תדהם [..]

15 ‏[..............]

[1]May my lord, the governor[f] hear [2]the appeal of his servant.

Your servant [3]is a reaper working in [4]Hazar-asam. Your servant finished his harvest [5]and stored it a few days before stopping.[8] [6]After your servant had finished storing the harvest [7]a few days ago, Hoshayahu son of Shobay came [8]and took your servant's garment. After I finished [9]my harvesting a few days ago, he took your servant's garment.

[10]All my companions who were harvesting with me in the heat [11]of the [sun] will testify for me. They will testify that what I have said is true. I am innocent of [12]any [offense.]

[So please return] my garment. If the governor does not consider it his obligation to [13]have [your servant's garment] sent back, [do] it [14]out of pity! You must not remain silent [when [15]your servant is without his garment.]

Petition of a Widow

50a. Moussaïeff Hebrew Ostracon #2
(second half of seventh century B.C.E. [?])

1 ‏יבֹרֹ[כך [.] יהוה בשֹלֹ[ם . ועת . ישמ-

2 ‏ע . אדני . הֹשֹר] את אמתֹרֹ] מת

3 ‏אישי . לא בנם . והיה . ידך .

4 ‏עמי . ונתתה . ביד . אמתך . את . ה-

5 ‏נחלה אשר . דברתה . לעמס-

6 ‏יהו . ואת . שדה . החטם . אש-

7　ר בנעמה . נתתה . לאח-

8　. יו

[1]May YHWH bless you in peace!

[2]May my lord the governor hear your maidservant.

[3]My husband died with no children.[h] I ask that you would exercise your authority [4]on my behalf and grant your maidservant [5]the estate of which you spoke to [6]Amasyahu.[i]

You have already given the wheat field [7-8]in Naamah to his brother.[j]

A Royal Order concerning Silver for the Temple

50b. Moussaïeff Hebrew Ostracon #1
(second half of seventh century B.C.E. [?])

1　כאשר צוך . אשי-

2　הו . המלך . לתת . ביד

3　[ז]כריהו . כסף תר-

4　שש . לבית יהוה []

5　ש׳ 3

[1-2]As King Ashyahu has ordered you: [3-5]you are to turn over three shekels of top-grade silver[k] to [Ze]karyahu for the temple of YHWH.[l]

Notes

[a] On this word, see note f below.

[b] This identification seems probable, despite the difficulty of reconciling the two names etymologically, on which see Bordreuil, Israel, and Pardee 1996: 52; 1998: 4. On the basis of the name alone, the earlier Judahite king Joash/Jehoash (ca. 800–788) or his north-Israelite namesake (ca. 836–798) might be considered. There was even a prominent member of a priestly family named Zechariah in the time of Joash of Judah (2 Chr 24:20–22). McCarter argues in favor of identifying the ostracon's "Ashyahu" with this earlier Joash/Jehoash (McCarter 1999: 153–54 and 323 n. 47). The question of date depends on paleographic considerations as well as the etymology of the name of the king in question. The paleographic evidence is difficult to evaluate. Many of the letters do appear, as McCarter notes, to be typologically more archaic than would be expected for a late seventh-century text. But there are also some apparent late features. I am provisionally following the date proposed by the original editors of the text, but certainty is not possible.

[c] McCarter (1999: 153–54 and 323 n. 47) also expresses his caution on the question of authenticity, mainly because the texts were not found in a controlled excavation, but he eventually treats them as apparently genuine.

[d] Christopher Rollston, in an e-mail dated November 15, 2002, summarized the technical evidence leading him to this conclusion: (1) the lab tests were not actually "double-blind"; (2) "modern contaminants" detected beneath the patina of the ostraca, originally interpreted by him as accidental contamination due to imperfect handling and storage, could also be interpreted as evidence that the ostraca were produced within the past few decades; (3) "a patina like the one on the ostraca could be produced today by a trained technician with access to the right compounds." In addition, he draws attention to the mixed paleographic forms noted in note b. While Rollston's technical reasons are not evidence of forgery, but only of the *possibility* of forgery, the anomalous forms in the script are not easily dismissed. Rollston and others are continuing to study the question, and it must be admitted that the jury is still out on the authenticity question.

[e] Pardee (2002: 86) convincingly refutes the most serious objections raised by Eph'al and Naveh and states emphatically his continuing conviction that the texts are authentic. "To believe the opposite requires the hypothesis that the forger was a master epigrapher, a master grammarian (only a skilled Hebraist could have produced a text that so perfectly reflects the intricacies of Biblical Hebrew morpho-syntax), a master of biblical law, and a master chemist (capable of producing ancient ink and an ancient patina [citing Rollston 1998, on which see note d above]). The forger would also ... have had to be cunning enough to produce some unexpected forms such as {whyh ydk 'my} (line 3)."

[f] In the first edition, I translated "commander," but Bordreuil, Israel, and Pardee (1998: 9) have argued persuasively that *śar* does not imply a military commander in this text and that the frequent assumption that the appeal was written in a situation of military occupation is unfounded.

[g] Or "before Sabbath."

[h] Or "sons." It seems to have been common practice in biblical Israel for the male offspring to inherit the property of a deceased father. But there is narrative evidence that in exceptional cases, a daughter could also inherit (Num 27:1–11).

[i] If Amasyahu is not the deceased husband but some other interested individual (see introductory comments above), this phrase could be translated, "the estate that you had promised to Amasyahu."

[j] Alternatively, *nttb* can be read as a virtual command form, a special use of the perfect called "precative" (see Waltke and O'Connor 1990: 494). In this case, the sentence could be translated "And would you give the wheat field ... to his brother."

[k] Literally, "silver of Tarshish." Tarshish, perhaps to be identified with Spain, was known in antiquity as a source of fine silver (Jer 10:9; cf. 1 Kgs 10:22; 2 Chr 9:21; Ezek 27:12; 38:13). Elsewhere in the ancient Near East, it was common when making payment in silver bullion to specify the grade of silver (Dandamaev 1984b: 58–59).

[l] Or perhaps "[...] just as King A. has ordered you. You are to turn over" (etc.). The Hebrew syntax of the first clause is odd, and the authors of the *editio principes* suggest that the ostracon may originally have been part of a dossier in which it was preceded by at least one other related text (Bordreuil, Israel, and Pardee 1996: 50; 1998: 4).

VII

Judean Military-Administrative Letters from Arad and Lachish

THIS CHAPTER CONTAINS TWO collections of military letters in Hebrew from the last days of the Judean monarchy. Originating in Arad, the letters in the first group (nos. 51–60) date mostly to around 597 B.C.E. The second group, from Lachish (nos. 61–67), is probably to be dated about eight years later. These letters, together with the biblical accounts of the campaigns of Nebuchadnezzar and the Babylonian Chronicle (Wiseman 1956), give us more thorough documentation of these years than for any comparable period in ancient Israel's history.

By the late seventh century, the Neo-Assyrian Empire was on the verge of collapse. Nineveh fell in 612 to a coalition of Babylonians and Medes. A few Assyrian troops under Ashur-uballit II resisted for three more years, but by 609, the year of Josiah's death (2 Kgs 23:29; 2 Chr 35:20–24), the last vestiges of Assyrian power had been crushed. For the next half century, the new imperial power in Mesopotamia was to be Babylonia.

In Judah, Josiah's son Jehoahaz (Shallum) was crowned in 609 in his father's place. But the Egyptian Pharaoh Neco (609–594), ever eager to intervene in Judean affairs, replaced him with his brother Jehoiakim (also called Eliakim [609–598]; see 2 Kgs 23:31–35), and for several years Egypt was the power behind the Judean throne. Egyptian troops remained in Syria, while the Babylonians under King Nabopolassar and young Prince Nebuchadnezzar consolidated their power closer to home.

In 605 Nebuchadnezzar brought his armies back to Syria and met the Egyptians head on, dealing them a decisive defeat at Carchemish and again near Hamath. In August, he returned home to assume the throne on the death of his father, but by late the next year he was back, leading his forces down the Philistine coast (cf. Jer 47 and the Babylonian Chronicle). King Adon's futile appeal to Egypt for assistance (no. 2) dates from this time. Meanwhile, Jehoiakim switched his allegiance from Egypt to Babylonia.

In the winter of 601–600, Nebuchadnezzar tried to invade Egypt but met such stiff resistance that he was compelled to draw back to Babylonia to regroup, prompting Jehoiakim to rebel. For three years, until Nebuchadnezzar was able to return to the west, he kept the Judeans off balance by harassing them with armed bands of Moabites, Ammonites, and Arameans, supported by a few Babylonian army units still in the area. In the eastern Negev, cross-border raids from Edom became more and more common (nos. 53–54).

In December 598 the expected Babylonian retribution came, and Jerusalem was besieged. Jehoiakim died suddenly, either in defense of the city or at the hands of an assassin. His young son Jehoiachin surrendered in March 597 and, along with many of the leading people in the land, was carried away to Babylonia.

The following years were chaotic, with successive attempts by Judean nationalists to gain independence and punitive measures by the Babylonians to reassert their authority. Around 589, Judah rebelled again, hoping for support from Egypt, where Hophra (Apries, 589–570) had just ascended the throne.

Once more the Babylonians marched on Judah and blockaded Jerusalem (in early 588 or a year later). Jerusalem was cut off for eighteen months, with only one brief respite when the Babylonians had to withdraw to repel an Egyptian force from the south. One by one the other fortifications in Judah were taken, Lachish and Azekah being the last to hold out. By this time, Jerusalem had been reduced to desperate straits by famine, and in July 587 the Babylonians breached the city wall. Jerusalem was captured, looted, and razed. Top officials were executed, and many more were taken away by their conquerors. The Babylonian exile had begun.

Arad, the site where the first group of letters in this chapter were found, was a city in the eastern Negev, roughly halfway between Beersheba and the Dead Sea, near the modern town of the same name. The oldest remains of the settlement date from the Early Bronze Age. During the Israelite monarchy, Arad's border location, astride the trails leading up the wadis from Edom into southern Judah, gave it particular strategic importance. A stone fortification tower, some fifty meters square, was erected during the time of the united monarchy. Over succeeding centuries this citadel was repeatedly destroyed and rebuilt, down to the time of the Romans. Israeli and American archaeologists digging at Arad from 1962 to 1967 uncovered twelve strata from the Israelite period and later.

In the late monarchic period, the time of these letters, Arad was a fortified supply depot. Staple foods were stockpiled and sent on demand to Judean army units stationed throughout the region. It also served as a troop transit point (see no. 53). Archaeological evidence indicates that the fortress fell temporarily into Egyptian hands in 609. The Egyptians confiscated the supplies in the warehouse and then burned the citadel. Two inventories of foodstuffs, one in hieratic Egyptian, the other in Hebrew, probably date from this incident (Aharoni 1981: 61–64).

Shortly thereafter, probably in 604, when Babylonia was on the move and the Egyptians no longer could maintain their influence, the fort was rebuilt by Judah on the same general plan as before. The new citadel stood only about a decade. In 597, while Nebuchadnezzar's army was invading Judah from the north, the fortress was captured and destroyed again, apparently by raiders from Edom.

The excavators of Arad found over a hundred Hebrew inscriptions and ostraca, most of them fragmentary, dating from the ninth century to the early sixth century B.C.E. Twenty-one or twenty-two ostraca can be identified as letters, of which nine are included here.

Unresolved questions remain concerning stratigraphy and dating (Aharoni 1981: 9, 70–74; Holladay 1976: 275, 281 n. 26; Pardee 1978b: 323 n. 144; 1982: 28), but most of the letters were written between the beginning of Josiah's reign and the final capture of Jerusalem by Babylonia. Numbers 53–60 are generally dated to early 597, just before Jehoiachin surrendered Jerusalem. Number 52, found on the surface, seems slightly earlier. Number 51 is still earlier, going back to the latter years of Manasseh (687/686–642), the time of Amon (642–640), or the earlier years of Josiah (640–609).

Two distinct types of letters are found at Arad. First, there is official military correspondence—orders and reports concerning such matters as troop disposition (no. 53) and intelligence (no. 51; see also nos. 52 and 54). Second, there are notes concerning the issue and dispatch of rations (nos. 55–60).

A recurrent motif is the threat from Edom. Number 51 alludes to intelligence reports from Edom. Number 53 is an urgent order from the king (Jehoiakim or Jehoiachin) to reinforce the Judean garrison at nearby Ramat-Negev (Horvat ʿUza?; see Josh 19:8; 1 Sam 30:27) against the Edomites (Aharoni 1981: 146–48; otherwise Lemaire 1977: 192). Number 52 is apparently a letter from a new king of Judah, possibly Jehoahaz (609) or Jehoiakim (609–598).

Numbers 55–60 are requisitions from commanders in other locations, authorizing the release and transport of grain, flour, dough, bread, wine, vinegar, and olive oil, with occasional appended notes on other topics (see nos. 56–58). One contains a cryptic allusion to a man who has taken up residence (possibly asylum) in the temple at Jerusalem (no. 55). No other ancient Hebrew documents except this one and no. 50b refer to the First Temple. There are frequent references to "Greeks" (Hebrew *kittiyyîm*, a word used centuries later at Qumran to refer to Romans),[a] either

Greek mercenaries in the service of Judah or itinerant middlemen who distributed supplies.

The person most often named in the requisitions is Elyashib ben Eshyahu, chief supply officer at Arad. Modern writers often refer to him as commander of the fortress, but it is not certain that his responsibilities went beyond those of a quartermaster. Letters 55–60 were found in the ruins of Elyashib's office. Three seals from a slightly earlier stratum and several other documents also bear his name. Elyashib evidently held his post before the citadel was taken by Egypt in 609 and returned to his command when it was rebuilt in 604.

The letters from Lachish (nos. 61–67) provide a fragmentary but unparalleled picture of the day-to-day concerns of a Judean officer on the eve of the Babylonian attack in 587. They also reflect the factionalism and political maneuvering in the capital at the time.

Lachish is situated in the Judean Shephelah, midway along an ancient road leading from Ashkelon on the coast to Hebron. Like Arad, Lachish was a royal fortress built on the ruins of a more ancient town. But whereas Arad was a fortified storehouse with a citadel of no great size, Lachish was an immense walled bastion, the greatest fortified city in Judah after Jerusalem.

Long before these letters were written, when Sennacherib of Assyria invaded Judah in 701, Lachish had played a key role in the defense of the nation. At that time, the city fell only after a protracted siege and a massed assault by Assyrian heavy armor. Sennacherib had his propaganda artists depict the siege on stone reliefs, which he displayed in his palace at Nineveh. The evident pride the Assyrian monarch took in the capture of Lachish indicates just how difficult a feat it was.

When Nebuchadnezzar besieged Jerusalem in early 588/587, Lachish once again played a significant role in the defense of Judah. According to Jer 34:6–7, it was one of the last two fortresses to fall before the capital itself.

The site of Lachish, modern Tell ed-Duweir, was excavated in the 1930s. A collection of Hebrew ostraca, mostly letters, was unearthed in the remains of the level destroyed in 587/586. Sixteen were found in a single room, thought to be a guard room, just inside the main entry gate at the southwest corner of the city wall.

Of the seven letters translated here, six are from the guard room. Number 65 was found under the surface of a later roadway but is contemporary with the other six. Their content is varied, but the letters are similar in style and tone, often using variants of the same formulas and clichés. The epistolary style is rather different from that of the Arad letters, suggesting writers trained in two different scribal traditions.

The Lachish letters were written over a very short span of time. Numbers 61 and 64 are actually written on pieces of the same broken pot. The most likely date is the summer of 588/587. The Babylonian invasion is imminent, but there is no hint that the Chaldean armies are actually in the land. On the contrary, it is still possible to travel unimpeded from Lachish to Jerusalem ("the city," no. 63), to Egypt (no. 62), and to the countryside for harvest (no. 66; on the dating see Pardee 1982: 77, 98).

Several thorny issues relating to the interpretation of these letters remain unresolved. Without entering into the debates, I simply state the assumptions made here: (1) Tell ed-Duweir is ancient Lachish; (2) these ostraca are copies or drafts of letters sent from (not to) Lachish (see Yadin 1984);[b] (3) the addressee, Yaush, named only in nos. 61, 62, and 64, is the intended recipient of most or all of the other letters; (4) Yaush is probably located in Jerusalem; (5) Hoshayahu, named as the sender of no. 62, is the author of the entire collection. These assumptions provide a coherent framework in which to read the letters.

Hoshayahu's exact position at Lachish is not certain, but his primary responsibilities relate to communication, in particular the collection and evaluation of military intelligence. He receives written reports from Jerusalem and elsewhere, which he sometimes returns without comment (no. 66) and sometimes subjects to a cutting analysis, evaluating their political and military implications (no. 64). In turn, he reports on matters that he presumes are not known to his superior in Jerusalem (no. 62). He also reports on the execution of previous orders (no. 63; see 61) and once requests orders when none have been received (no. 67). Military couriers appear to have carried messages to and from the capital at least once daily.

The allusion to a signal fire in no. 63 evidently refers to a military communications system. It has recently been suggested that the Lachish light was part of a comprehensive network of signal beacons linking the fortresses of the Judean Shephelah with Jerusalem (Mazar 1981). Given the probable date of the letters, the phrase "we cannot see Azekah" is not, as some interpreters have held, a reference to the fall of that city but is to be understood in the context of testing the signal system and training soldiers to use it prior to the arrival of the invasion forces.

The Lachish letters reflect the personality of their author more clearly than any other group in this collection. Hoshayahu comes across as a crusty, blunt-speaking, professional soldier, confident of his own ability and utterly tactless in the face of authority. He is given to emotional outbursts, sarcasm, and heavy-handed irony. This is especially evident in his repeated use of the phrase "I am nothing but a dog." The phrase is a traditional formula of self-abasement in the presence of greater authority. But Hoshayahu, although outranked by Yaush ("my lord"), is not in the least cowed by his superior, as is clear from his angry outburst when Yaush impugns his ability to read (no. 62). Hoshayahu's insubordinate criticism of royal officials in Jerusalem, possibly all the way up to the king himself (no. 64), is reminiscent of the complaints of many a line officer in later times, convinced that the politicians are ruining the conduct of the war. Hoshayahu and Yaush appear as "hardliners" who want to avoid any statements by national leaders that would undermine troop morale.

A Report from Edom

51. Arad 40 (IM 67–631)
(second half of seventh century B.C.E.)

בנכם . גמר[יהו] ונח-   1

מיהו . שלח[ו לשלם]   2

מלכיהו ברכתך ליהו[ה   3

ועת . הטה [ע]בדך ל[לבה   4

אל . אשר אמ[רת וכתבת]י   5

אל אדני [את כל אשר ר-]   6

צה . האיש [ואשיהו ב-]   7

א . מאתך . ואיש] לא נתן ל[-   8

הם . והן . ידעתה [המכתבם מ-]   9

אדם . נתתם לאדנ[י בטרם י-]   10

רד ים . וא[ש]י[ו]הו . ל[ן בביתי]   11

והא . המכתב . בקש [ולא נתת-]   12

י . ידע . מלך . יהוד[ה כי אי-]   13

ננו . יכלם . לשלח . את ה[....]וז-   14

את הרעה אש[ר] אד[ם עשתה]   15

[1]Your son[c] Gemar[yahu] and Nehemyahu [2]send [greetings] to [3]Malkiyahu. I bless [you by YHWH].

[4]Your servant has applied himself [5]to what you ordered. [I am] writing [6]to my lord [everything that] [7]the man wanted.

[Ashyahu has] come [8]from you, but [he has not given] them any men. [9]You know [the reports from] [10]Edom. I sent them to [my] lord [before] [11]evening. Ashyahu is staying [in my house]. [12]He tried to obtain the report, [but I would not give it to him].

[13]The king of Judah should be told [that] we [are unable] [14]to send [...].[d] [This is] [15]the evil that the Edomites [have done].

A Royal Fragment

52. Arad 88 (Arad Excav. Reg. No. 7904/1)ᶜ
(609 B.C.E. [?])

1　אני . מלכתי . בכ]ל ארץ ישראל[
2　אמץ . זרע . ו].....[
3　מלך . מצרים . ל].....[

[1]I have become king in all [the land of Israel]. [2]Be strong and [...] [3]the king of Egypt to [...].

Orders from the King

53. Arad 24 (IM 72–121)
(597 B.C.E.)

A

1　אֺל].................[
2　אלישבֹ].............[
3　לס].....[מלך .].[במ].......[
4　].......[חיל].........[
5　].......[כס]..........[
6　].......[עבד].........[
7　].......[ט].....[ר].....[
8　].......[וע]..........[
9　].......[וכ].........[
10　].................[
11　].................[

B

12　מערד 50 ומקינ]ה].......[
13　ה . ושלחתם . אתם . רמת / נג]ב בי-[
14　ד . מלכיהו בן קרבאור והב-
15　קידם . על . יד . אלישע בן ירמי-

16   הו ברמת / נגב . פן . יקרה . את ה-

17   עיר . דבר . ודבר המלך אתכם

18   בנבשכם . הנה שלחתי להעיד

19   בכם . הים . האנשם את . אליש-

20   ע . פן . תבא . אדם . שמה

¹To [...] ²Elyashib [...].

³[...] king [...] ⁴[...] army [...] ⁵⁻⁶[...] servant [...]. ⁷⁻¹¹[*illegible*]

[...] ¹²fiftyᶠ from Arad, and [...] from Qinah [...]. ¹³Send them to Ramat-Negev [under] the command of ¹⁴Malkiyahu son of Qerabur. He is to ¹⁵hand them over to Elisha son of Yirmeyahu ¹⁶at Ramat-Negev, so that nothing will happen to the ¹⁷city.

This is an order from the king— ¹⁸a life-and-death matter for you. I am sending you this message to warn ¹⁹you now: these men *must* be with Elisha ²⁰in case the Edomites come!

Fragmentary Letter

54. Arad 21 (IM 72–126)
(597 B.C.E.)

1   בנך . יהוכל . שלח . לשלם . גדליהו [בן]

2   אליאר . ולשלם . ביתך ברכתך . ל[יהו-]

3   ה . ועת . הן . עשה . אדני . [......]

4   [......]ישלם . יהוה . לאדנ[י...]

5   [.........]אדם] . [חי]הْوה.........]

6   [.........][ה][....][עת].............]

7   [.........]וכל אשר[................]

8   [....] ואם . עود[..............]

9   [.....]אש[........................]

10 [....][לח].......................]

¹Your son Yehukal sends greetings to Gedalyahu [son of] ²Elyair and your household!

I bless you by [YHWH].

³If my lord has done [...] ⁴[...], may YHWH reward [my] lord [...]. ⁵[...] Edom [...] by God [...] ⁶⁻⁷[...] whatever [...] ⁸[...] and if [there is?] still [...]. ⁹⁻¹¹[*illegible*]

Rations and Other Matters

55. Arad 18 (IM 67–669)
(597 B.C.E.)

A

אל אדני . אלי- 1

שב . יהוה יש- 2

אל לשלמך . ועת 3

תן . לשמריהו 4

√ . ולקרסי 5

תתן . Ⱶ ולד- 6

בר . אשר . צ- 7

ותני . שלם . 8

בית . יהוה 9

B

הא . ישב 10

[1]To my lord Elyashib:
[2]May YHWH [3]bless you.
[4]Issue Shemaryahu [5]half a donkey-load of flour(?).[g] And give the Qerosite[h] [6]a full donkey-load.
As for the [7]matter about which [8]you gave me orders—all is well.[i] [9–10]He is staying in the temple of YHWH.[j]

56. Arad 1 (IM 67–713)
(597 B.C.E.)

אל . אלישב . ו- 1

עת . נתן לכתים 2

יין . ב′ 3 ו- 3

כתב . שם / הים . 4

ומעוד . הקמח 5

הראשון . ת- 6

7   קמח . 1 ⊢ . רכב

8   ל- . להם . לעשת

9   . מיין . חם

10   האגנת . תתן

[1]To Elyashib:

[2]Issue the Greeks [3]three large jugs[k] of wine and [4]record the date. [5-6]Take some of what's left of the old flour,[l] and [7]have a donkey-load of it loaded up for them [8]to make bread. [9-10]Give them some of the wine from the big bowls.

57. Arad 2 (IM 67–625)
(597 B.C.E.)

1   ל- / נתן . ועת . אלישב . אל

2   -ל . יין 2 ׳ב . כתים

3   -ו הימם / ארבעת

4   -ו לחם 300

5   -וה יין . החמר . מלא

6   . תאחר / אל . מחר סבת

7   -ונת . חמץ . עוד . ואם

8   . להם . ת

[1]To Elyashib:

Issue [2]the Greeks two jugs of wine for [3]the four days, [4]three hundred loaves of bread, and [5]a full donkey-load of wine.

[6]Deliver tomorrow—don't be late! [7-8]And if there is any more vinegar, give it to them.

58. Arad 3 (IM 67–623)
(597 B.C.E.)

A

1   . ועת . אלישב . אל

2   -ו . ׳ב 3 . היין . מן . תן

3   -ב על . חנניהו . צוך

4   -צ משא . עם שבע / אר

מד . חמרם . וצררת   5

אתם . בצק . ו-   6

ספר . החטם והל-   7

חם ולקחת   8

B

אלכמׄ[...............]   9

רי[.................]   10

ל[.................]   11

ואדמם . ה [........]   12

[...................]   13

[..].מׄ[..............]   14

¹To Elyashib:

²Issue three jugs of wine to bearer.

³Hananyahu hereby orders you to ⁴⁻⁵Beersheba with a double donkey-load:ᵐ Fix ⁶them up with a consignment of dough.ⁿ

⁷⁻⁸Take inventory of the wheat, and count the loaves of bread. Take [...].

⁹⁻¹⁴[*rest illegible, except for the phrase* "and the Edomites."]

59. Arad 17 (IM 67–624)
(597 B.C.E.)

A

אל . נחם . [ו]עת ב-   1

א ביתה . אלישב .   2

בן אשיהו . ולקח-   3

ת . משם 1 . שמן . ו-   4

שלח . ל[.] [..] מהרה . ו-   5

חתם . אתה בח-   6

תמך   7

B

ב 24 לחדש נתן נחם ש-   8

מן ביד הכתי . 1   9

[1]To Nahum:
[2]Go to the house of Elyashib [3]son of Ashyahu. Get [4]one measure[o] of oil from there, and [5]send it immediately to [...].[p] [6]Seal it with [7]your seal.

Endorsement (in another hand): [8]On the twenty-fourth of the month, Nahum handed over [9]the oil to the Greek for delivery: one measure.

60. Arad 16 (IM 67–990)
(597 B.C.E.)

1	אחך . חנניהו . שלח / לשל-
2	ם אלישב . ולשלם ביתך בר-
3	כתך ליהוה . ועת כצאתי
4	מביתך ושלחתי את
5	ה[כ]סף 8 ש׳ לבני גאליהו . [ב-]
6	י[ד עז]ריהו ואת [......]
7	[...] אתך וה[......]
8	את כסף[.....][ואם ...]
9	[.]צבכ[.....][שלח.....]
10	את נחם ולא תשלח ל[.....]

[11–12 *faint traces only*]

[1]Your brother Hananyahu sends greetings to [2]Elyashib and your household. [3]I bless you by YHWH!

When I leave [4]your house, I will send[q] [5]the money (eight shekels) to the sons of Gealyahu [6]by Azaryahu, as well as the [...] [7][...] with you (?). So [...] [8]the money, and if [...] [9][...] send [...] [10]Nahum, but don't send[r] [...]. [11–12]*[remainder illegible]*

Greetings to a Superior Officer

61. Lachish 2 (BM 125 702)
(589 B.C.E.)

1	אל אדני . יאוש ישמע
2	יהוה . את אדני . ש[מעת] של-
3	ם . עת / כים עת . כים מי . עבד-

4   ך כלב כי . זכר אדני . את .

5   ]ע[בדה . יבכר . יהוה את א-

6   ]רנ[י דבר . אשר לא . ידעתה

[1]To my lord Yaush.

[2]May YHWH send you good news [3]this very day!

I am nothing [4]but a dog; why should you should think [5]of me?[s] May YHWH help you find out [6]what you need to know!

Protest of Literacy, Troop Movements, etc.

62. Lachish 3 (IM 38–127)
(589 B.C.E.)

A

1   עבדך . הושעיהו . שלח . ל-

2   הגר לאדני יאוש . ישמע .

3   יהוה את אדני . שמעת . שלם

4   ושמעת . טב [.] ועת . הפקח

5   נא [.] את אזן [.] עבדך . לספר . אשר .

6   שלחתה [.] אל עבדך . אמש . כי . לב

7   עבדך דוה . מאז . שלחך . אל . עבד-

8   ך [.] וכי [.] אמר . אדני . לא . ידעתה .

9   קרא ספר חיהוה . אם . נסה . א-

10   יש לקרא לי . ספר לנצח . וגם .

11   כל ספר [.] אשר יבא . אלי [.] אם .

12   קראתי . אתה ועׄוׄד . אתננהו

13   אל . מאומה ולעבדך . הגד .

14   לאמר . ירד שר . הצבא

15   כניהו בן אלנתן לבא .

16   מצרימה . ואת

B

17   הורויהו בן אחיהו ו-

18   אנשו שלח לקחת . מזה

19   וספר . טביהו עבד . המלך . הבא

20   אל . שלם . בן ידע . מאת . הנבא . לאמ-

21   ר . השמר . שלחה . עב>ד<ך . אל . אדני

[1]A report from your servant Hoshayahu [2]to my lord Yaush.

May [3]YHWH send you good news [4]and prosperity!

Now then, would you please [5]explain to me[t] what you meant by the letter [6]you sent me last night? I've [7]been in a state of shock ever since I got it. [8]"Don't you know [9]how to read a letter?" you said. By God,[u] nobody ever had [10]to read *me* a letter! And [11]when I get a letter, once [12]I've read it, I can recite it back [13]verbatim, word for word!

I have just received [14]word that Commander [15]Konyahu son of Elnatan has moved south to enter [16]Egypt. He has sent to have [17]Hawduyahu[v] son of Ahiyahu and [18]his men transferred from here.

[19]I am sending a letter confiscated[w] by Tobyahu, the royal administrator. It was sent [20]to Shallum son of Yada from the prophet, saying, [21]"Beware!"

Report on Signal-Fire and Other Matters

63. Lachish 4 (IM 38–128)
(589 B.C.E.)

A

1   ישמע . יהו]ה את אדנ]י עת כים .

2   שמעת טב . ועת ככל אשר . שלח אדני .

3   כן . עשה . עבדך כתבתי על הדלת ככל .

4   אשר שלח]תה א]לי . וכי . שלח א-

5   דני . על . דבר בית / הרפד אין . שם א-

6   דם וסמכיהו לקחה . שמעיהו ו-

7   יעלהו . העירה ועבדך . אינ-

8   י].[ש]לח שמה את העד] הים]

B

9   כי אם . בתסבת . הבקר]י]ב]א]

10   וידע . כי אל . משאת לכש . נח-

11 נו שמרם . ככל . האתת . אשר נתן

12 אדני . כי לא ֯ נראה את עז-

13 קה

[1]May YHWH send you good news this very day!

[2-3]I have carried out all of your orders and have kept a written record of them:[x]

[4-5]On the matter you spoke of regarding Beth-*hrpd*:[y] there is no one there.

[6]Regarding Semakyahu: Shemayahu has arrested him and [7]had him taken up to the city. I cannot [8]send the witness there today, [9]but he will come sometime tomorrow morning.[z]

[10-11]You should know that we are tending the signal-fire of Lachish according to the code you gave us,[aa] [12-13]for we cannot see Azekah.

Morale

64. Lachish 6 (IM 38–129)
(589 B.C.E.)

1 אל אדני יאוש . ירא ֗ . יהוה א-

2 ת ֗ אדני את העת הזה . שלם מי

3 עבדך ֗ כלב כי . שלח . אדני א[ת ספ-]

4 ר המלך [ואת] ספרי השר[ם לאמ-]

5 ר קרא נא והנה . דברי . ה[שרם]

6 לא טבם לרפת ידיך [ולהש]

7 קט . ידי האנ[שם...][יד]ע[...]

8 [.....][אנכ]י [אדני הלא תכ-]

9 תב אל[יהם] לא[מ]ר למ[ה תעשו] .

10 כזאת ו[....][שלם...][הל-]

11 מלך [......][ו].[.]ר[..]

12 [.]א[....][חי . יהוה אלה-]

13 יך כי מ[אז קרא עב-]

14 דך את הספרם לא היה

15 לעב[ד]ך [........]

¹To my lord Yaush.

May YHWH make ²this time a good one for you.

³I am nothing but a dog; why should you should send me ⁴the letters from the king and the officials and ask me ⁵to read them?

What the officials say ⁶is not good. It will undermine your authority and ⁷the morale of the troops. [...] ⁸[...] you. Won't you write ⁹them to inquire, "Why are you doing ¹⁰this?" [...] peace(?) [...] Does ¹¹the king have(?) [. . .]? ¹²[. . .] I swear to God,ᵇᵇ ¹³since I read ¹⁴the letters, I have not had ¹⁵[a moment's peace!]

Fragment Mentioning a Prophet

65. Lachish 16 (BM 125 706)
(589 B.C.E.)

A

[....]חמ[.̊...]	1
[....] ה הי[....]	2
[....]שׁלח / הע[....]	3
[....] ס]פֹּר . בני[...]	4
[....] י̊]הו הנבא[...]	5
[....]מ[..]	6

B

[....]א[.....]	7
[....̊]ע[...]	8
[....]א שלח[....]	9
[....]ה̊]בר וח[...]	10

¹⁻²[...] ³[...] send the [...] ⁴[... the] letter of the sons of [...]ᶜᶜ ⁵[... -ya]hu the prophet [...] ⁶⁻⁸[*illegible*] ⁹[...] send [...] ¹⁰[...] word and [...].

Rations

66. Lachish 5 (BM 125 703)
(589 B.C.E.)

1   ישמע |יהוה את אד|ני

2 |שמעת שלו|ם וטב |עת|

3 |כים עת כי|ם֯ מי . עבדך

4   כלב . כי . |ש|לחתה אל עבד-

5   ך . א|ת| הס֯|פרם כ|זא-

6 |ת| ֯ . השב . עבדך . הספר-

7   ם . אל אדני . יראך י-

8   הוה ֯ . הקצר ֯ . בטב֯

9   הים . האל . עבדך . י<>ב<א

10   טביהו . זרע למלך

[1]May YHWH send you, my lord, [2]the very best possible news [3]this very day!
I am nothing [4]but a dog; why have you sent me [5]these letters? [6]I am returning them [7]to you.

I pray that [8]YHWH will let you see a good harvest [9]today. Is Tobyahu going to send me [10]some of the king's grain?

67. Lachish 9 (BM 125 705)
(589 B.C.E.)

A

1   ישמע יהוה ֯ . את אד-

2   ני ש|מעת| שלם . ו|טב|

3 |וע|ת תן לחם 10 ו-

4 |יי|ן 2 השב֯

5   א|ת| עבדך ד-

6   בר ב-

B

7   יד שֵׁלֹמֹיהו . א-

8   שר נעשה . מ-

9   חר

[1]May YHWH send you, my lord, [2]the very best possible news.

[3]Please issue ten loaves of bread and [4]two jugs[dd] of wine to bearer.

Send [5-6]me word back [7]by Shelemyahu [8]as to what we are to do [9]tomorrow.

Notes

[a] For instance, 1QM i.2, 4, 6, 9, etc. (*War Scroll*). In addition to the *War Scroll* (1Q33, 4Q471, 4Q491–497) and *War Rule* (4Q285), the word occurs in the *pesharim* on Habakkuk (1QpHab), Nahum (4Q169), Isaiah[a] (4Q161), and Psalms (1Q16). For details on Qumran usage, see Lim 2000.

[b] Yadin's additional suggestion that these are alternative drafts written in preparation for sending a smaller number of letters is much less convincing.

[c] Or "sons," reading *bnkm* as plural (Lemaire 1977: 207–8).

[d] Perhaps "fresh troops" from Arad to reinforce some other post.

[e] Renz (1995: 1:302–3) questions the identification of this ostracon as a letter, given its informal style and lack of epistolary formulas, considering it rather to be a scribal exercise or a copy of a royal inscription. But the royal donation text (no. 50b) shares the the same simple unformulaic style.

[f] Or possibly "five." The sign is not clear.

[g] The translation follows the interpretation of Pardee (1978b: no. 17; 1982: 55).

[h] One of the temple personnel (Levine 1969: 49–51).

[i] The sense seems to be, "It is taken care of," or "I have dealt with it."

[j] Only the temple in Jerusalem can be meant. At an earlier time there was a small temple in Arad, but it had been destroyed before this letter was written.

[k] Literally, "baths"; see the glossary. The total ration called for is approximately 120 to 135 liters (32–36 gallons).

[l] Literally, "from what is left of the first flour." If this does mean the oldest, and if the Greeks themselves brought the note to Arad, it implies that they could not understand it. Whether the "wine from the big bowls (or 'craters')" was also second-rate, we do not know. Wine could not be stored for any extended time in such large vessels. Perhaps the wine was watered in accordance with Greek taste (Pardee 1982: 32).

[m] So, following Pardee 1982: 35. The translation "a pair of pack donkeys" (Gogel 1998: 386) does not fit the Hebrew syntax so well.

[n] I have followed Pardee (1982: 35) in taking the literal sense to be "bind them up with dough." A less likely alternative yields "hurry them on, without letting up" (Lemaire mentions this possibility without accepting it [1977: 165]; cf. Smelik 1991: 109).

[o] One *bath?*

[p] Aharoni (1981: 32, 34) and Pardee (1982: 51–52) restore the place-name "Ziph." No word can be seen in the photograph, though Aharoni claimed to see faint traces on the original. Others restore l[hm] "to them" (Renz 1995: 1:381 n. 7).

[q] This revised translation follows the recent suggestion of Gogel 1998: 263 that the verb be analyzed as perfect with *waw* consecutive following the infinitive.

[r] Or "and he will not send," reading *yšlk* (Renz 1995: 1:380).

[s] Literally, "Who is your servant but a dog, that my lord should remember his servant?" See also nos. 64 and 66 and 2 Kgs 8:13.

[t] Literally, "open the ear (?) of your servant." An alternative reading is "open the *eye*," *'yn* (Renz 1995: 1:417).

[u] Literally, "As YHWH lives, if...." In the highly emotional style of this letter, the conventional expression takes on a tone close to profanity.

[v] On the vocalization of the name, see Renz 1995: 2/1:65. The form "Hodawya(hu)" (Hodaviah) occurs in the Hebrew Bible.

[w] The context implies that the letter was seized as subversive material. The text literally says only, "a letter of T."

[x] Literally, "I have written them on the door [*dlt*]." The last word may refer to a column of a papyrus roll or tablet (Renz 1995: 1:422).

[y] Neither the pronunciation nor the location of this place is known.

[z] Understanding *btsbt hbqr* as "in the course of the morning," and joining the phrase to the preceding clause, contrary to my translation in the first edition. See Renz 1995: 1:422 n. 1, on the passage.

[aa] Or "just as you ordered."

[bb] Literally, "As YHWH your God lives."

[cc] Or "my son's letter."

[dd] Probably "*baths*" is implied (Pardee 1982: 106; see the wine rations mentioned in nos. 56–58).

VIII

Fragmentary and Miscellaneous

THE FINAL CHAPTER contains an eclectic group of letters and fragments with little in common. They were written in different languages at different periods. The first few fragments (nos. 67a–b) are Hebrew; three letters are written in other Canaanite languages (nos. 68–70); and two recently published ones are in Aramaic (nos. 71–72).

In the mid-1970s, an Israeli archaeological team excavated an ancient caravan stopover site at Kuntillet ʿAjrûd, a remote spot in the northern Sinai Peninsula (Meshel and Meyers 1976). Among the finds were two *pithoi,* large storage jars, dating from the late ninth or early eighth century B.C.E. These are covered with crudely executed drawings in red and black ink, and inscriptions, some of them of a distinctly religious character.

The inscriptions, still not definitively published (see the preliminary publication of Meshel 1978), are not easy to decipher and have proven to be extremely difficult to interpret. Particularly contentious have been several references to "YHWH and his *asherah,*" about which an extensive secondary literature has grown up. The debate has centered around the question whether the italicized word refers to (1) a cultic site, (2) a cult object (cf. especially the condemnation of the so-called "sacred poles," [*asherim,* singular *asherah* in Deut 7:5; 12:3; 16:21 and several other passages in the Hebrew Bible]), or (3) the Near Eastern goddess Asherah (1 Kgs 15:13; 18:19; 2 Kgs 21:7; 23:4, 7, and various extrabiblical inscriptions), either the name of the goddess or a common noun referring to YHWH's consort, that is, his particular *asherah.* The interpretation of the word as a proper divine name is unlikely—proper names in Hebrew are not modified by possessive pronouns—and a great many scholars have accepted some form of the last interpretation listed, a conclusion with far-reaching implications for understanding popular Israelite religion in the time of the divided monarchies.

For a judicious and carefully nuanced evaluation of the issues concerning the religious significance of these inscriptions and several others with similar wording, see Miller 2000: 29–43, 51–52, where additional bibliography may be found.[a] Miller treats the inscriptions under the heading "Heterodox Yahwism" and understands the word *asherah* to connote something less than an independent female deity but more than simply a religious object. He explains, "It may have been a cult object of Yahweh, but, if so, it was one that could be understood separately from Yahweh—and thus, potentially at least, as the consort of Yahweh." In it can be seen "a move toward the hypostatization of the feminine dimension of deity" (Miller 2000: 36), a move opposed by the Deuteronomistic tradition.

Only recently have scholars recognized that two of the inscriptions containing the phrase in question are epistolary greeting formulas (Renz 1995: 1:49; see above, introduction, V.B.), apparently written as practice exercises, which explains their inclusion here (no. 67a).

Number 67b is a fragment of a Hebrew letter found at Muraba'at in the Judean desert south of Qumran. It was written on papyrus in the late eighth or early seventh century B.C.E., making it the earliest actual letter to have survived (in part) from ancient Judah. The papyrus is a palimpsest, that is, a text that was partially erased in antiquity so it could be reused for writing something else. In this case the letter was the first (erased) text, and little remains of it beyond the opening formula.

Each of the three Canaanite letters is written in a different dialect: *Edomite* (no. 68), the language of the indigenous inhabitants of southern Transjordan during the biblical period; *Ammonite* (no. 69), the language of north central Transjordan around modern Amman; and *Phoenician* (no. 70), the language of the seafaring Canaanites of the Lebanese coast and their colonies around the Mediterranean.

No other Edomite, Ammonite, or Phoenician letters have been found. They do, however, have some broad generic similarities with one another and with the Aramaic and Hebrew letters in this collection. Nothing of the ancient Ammonite language has survived aside from a handful of short inscriptions (most of them mere fragments) and a few seals, to which we may add a few place names and personal names from the Bible and ancient Near Eastern epigraphic sources. The written remains of Edomite are even more sparse: a few barely decipherable ostraca, a number of seals, and some names. Number 68 is the only connected Edomite text of any sort known. Phoenician is much more extensively attested, but no. 70 is the only letter.

Written in similar scripts, Edomite and Ammonite appear to have differed from Hebrew mainly in matters of pronunciation and word formation. The finer points of difference are, of course, invisible behind the consonantal writing system. Phoenician diverged more greatly from these three, but probably not so greatly as to prevent mutual intelligibility.

The three Canaanite letters all relate to economic transactions, specifically to loans: the repayment of a loan of grain (no. 68), a pledge of grain (no. 69), and an overdue payment of a loan of silver (no. 70). Thousands of comparable economic texts are known in Akkadian.

Number 68 was found in 1983 at Horvat ʿUza in the eastern Negev. The site is less than six miles south-southeast of Arad. Some scholars have suggested that it is to be identified with the site called Ramat-Negeb in a Hebrew letter from Arad (no. 53). While this is uncertain, Horvat ʿUza was definitely on the fringes of Judean territory. The letter is roughly contemporary with the Arad letters. Unlike the Arad corpus, the Edomite note gives no hint of the border tensions of the time. Number 69, the Ammonite letter, was found at Tell el-Mazār in the central Jordan Valley (modern Jordan, near Deir ʿAllā) and is also a recent discovery.

The Phoenician letter (no. 70), written on a poorly preserved papyrus found at Saqqara, Egypt, has been known since the early 1940s. Most Phoenician inscriptions have been discovered either in the Lebanese homeland or in the Punic settlements of North Africa, but there is scattered evidence for the presence of Phoenicians in various centers along the Nile in the sixth and fifth centuries as far south as Abu Simbel. As with some of the Aramaic letters (see the introduction to ch. 2), it is unclear whether the familiar terms of address ("my sister," etc.) imply real kinship.

The last two letters (nos. 71–72) are Aramaic. During the past decade a great many previously unknown Aramaic ostraca have found their way onto the antiquities market. Few of these are letters, but a recent publication provides two new additions to this collection (Ephʿal and Naveh 1996: 88–91). The exact provenance of the two letters is unknown, and they are undated. The editors, however, judge that they probably originated in the Judean desert region, in the area known in Greco-Roman times as Idumea. Their probable date is late fourth century, making these the latest texts in this collection.

Neither text contains any address or introductory formulas, but their content marks them clearly as letters or drafts for letters. Number 71 concerns a debtor who has defaulted on a loan. The letter presupposes the following situation: a traveling businessman (referred to only as "the merchant") has borrowed a substantial sum of money from two unnamed lenders, whom we will call "A" and "B." A and B are temporarily in possession of two female slaves—possibly more, the grammar is ambiguous as to number—belonging to the merchant. Whether the slaves were left as collateral for the loan or were hired from the merchant in a separate transaction is unclear. Both types of transaction are known in the ancient Near East of this time and earlier.[b]

Against this background, A now writes to B that the merchant is refusing to pay his debt. A says that B may restore one of the merchant's slaves to him but asks B to retain custody of the other one (or ones) in lieu of payment of the debt.

Number 72 is short and to the point, though the detailed background is unknown. A person in a socially inferior position writes a correspondent in a position of authority ("my lord") requesting that a woman be released, perhaps from imprisonment (cf. no. 40).

Epistolary Formulas from Kuntillet ʿAjrûd

67a. Kuntillet ʿAjrûd Pithoi A and B[c]
(late ninth–early eighth century B.C.E.)

A [Meshel Cat. "First Pithos"]

1   אמר . א[...]ה [...]ה [..]ך . אמר . ליהל[לאל] וליועשה . ו[....→][d]

    ברכת . אתכם

2   ליהוה . שמרן . ולאשרתה .

B [Meshel Cat. "Second Pithos"]

    [אמֿר]

1   אֿ[ו] אמריו

2   מר / ל . אדני

3   [את]אֿ . השֿלֿם

4   -לי . ברכתך

5   [תמן] הוֿ[ה]

6   -יב . ולאשרתה

7   רך . וישמרך

8   [נ]אד . עם ויהי

9   [...]י[e]

A: [1][...] says, say to Yehalle[lel], Yoashah, and [...]: I bless you [2]by YHWH of Samaria[f] and his *asherah*.[g]

B: [1-2]Amaryaw [*says*], [2]say to my lord, [3]Are you well? [4]I bless you by [5]YHWH of [*Teman*][h] [6]and his *asherah*. [7]May he bless you and keep you, [8]and be with my lord [9][...].

A Papyrus Letter Fragment from Muraba'at

67b. *papMur 17* (*DJD* 2, 17a)
(late eighth–early seventh century B.C.E.)

1 ‏[אָמֹר.]...[יהו . לך .] שֹׁ[ל]ֹח . שלֹ[ח]ֹת . אֹת שלם ביתך

2 ‏ועת . אל . תשמֹ[עֹ] לֹ[כֹלֹ] [וֹ]דֹבֹר אֹשֹׁר יֹ[ד]בֹר . אליך .

3 ‏הֹפֹ]..[חסת

4 ‏[..] [..] וֹרֹעֹֹת

5 ‏[..] [..] אל דֹר [..]

[1][...]yahu says to you: I send greetings to your household.
[2]Pay no atten[tion] to [wh]at [... i]s telling you. [...] [3–5][*remainder illegible*]

An Edomite Note concerning Grain Delivery

68. Horvat 'Uza Edomite O.
(Eastern Negev; late seventh–early sixth century B.C.E.)

1 ‏אמֹר . למלך . אמר . לבלבל .

2 ‏השלם . את . והברכתך

3 ‏לקוס . ועת . תן . את . האכל

4 ‏אשר . עמֹר . אחאמה [...]

5 ‏והרם עֹ[ז]אל . על מזֹ[ו ...]

6 ‏[..] חמר . האכל

[1]A message from Lumalak[i] to Bulbul.
[2]Are you well? I bless you [3]by Qaus.
Send the feed-grain [4]that is owed to Ahamah [...], [5]and have Uzziel deliver it to the granary: [...] [6][...] *homers* of feed-grain.

An Ammonite Note concerning Grain

69. Tell el-Mazār Ammonite O. (Ost. No. 3, JUM 223/79)
(Tell el-Mazār, Jordan; 600–550 B.C.E.)

אמר פלט אמר לאחה לעבדא|ל| 1

שלם את ועת שע|ו|רת אתן   2

לך שערת לשבת . כער|בן| 3

וע֗ת תן לפלט א|חך| 4

|.| ישב בא |.| 5

[1]A message from Pelet to his brother Ebed-El.
[2]Are you well?
I am sending you some barley [3]to deposit as a pledge. [4]Now give it to your brother Pelet [5][...] who lives in [...].

A Phoenician Letter

70. Saqqara Phoenician Papyrus (Cairo, Eg. Mus.)
(late sixth century [?] B.C.E.)

A

אמר . לאחתי . ארשת . אמר . אחתך . בשא . ושלם את . אף אנך .   1
שלם . ברכתך . לב-

עלצפן . ולכל . אל . תחפנחס . יפעלך . שלם . אפקן . הכסף .   2
אש . שלחת . לי . ותנת-

ן . לי מש|ק|ל 3 |ר| . ה|...|ל . אתכ֗ר ע|.| ומלאת . על תפני . אית .   3
כל כ-

סף . אש לי . בֿך . ויתת . |אתٰי֗|בטח . ברד |.| אש אדע . במא|..|ת   4
וש-

לחת לי את ספר הנקת אש למי|..|כי   5

B

אל ארשת בת א|שٰמٰ|ני|תן| 6

[1]To my sister, from your sister Basu.

Are you well? I am.

I bless you by [2]Baal-Saphon and all the gods of Tahpanhes. May they keep you well!

I am still waiting for the money you sent me. [3]Now you need to pay me an additional 3 [...]. Then I can pay Tipni(?) all [4]the money I have.[j] [...]. [5]Send me the receipt which [...].

[6]*Address:* To Arishut daughter of Eshmunyaton.

An Aramaic Note concerning a Debt

71. IdumeaOstr 199
(late fourth century B.C.E.)

A

זבונא זי הקים למנתן לי כספא	1
לא יהב כן אמר לי למה מסחר	2
אנת באתרי כסף לא איתי וחבא	3
זי מהן⸢ן⸣זוף כסף זי שאר עלויה	4

B

מ׳ 1 מתאמר כזי חזין ⸢.⸣ לא	5
הקבלת לגבר⸤יא⸥ כען הן אתה	6
תמה הבו לה חדה מן עלימתה	7
ושאריתא בחב יהוי	8

[1]The merchant who contracted to pay me the money [2]has not done so. This is what he said to me: "Why should you stay in business [3]instead of me? There isn't any money." So the debt [4]for which he is obligated,[k] that is, the money he still owes, [5]is reckoned at 1 *mina*,[l] as it was previously.[m]

Do not [6]enter a complaint with the officials.[n] If he comes [7]there, give him one of his slave-girls, [8]but the other one shall remain in exchange for his debt.

An Aramaic Note concerning Release of a Woman

72. IdumeaOstr 196
(late fourth century B.C.E.)

1   הן על מראי

2   טב ישבקו

3   ברת חגי

[1]If it please my lord, [2-3]let the daughter of Haggai be released.

Notes

[a] A sampling of earlier discussion from different viewpoints can be found in Lemaire 1984; Dever 1984; Olyan 1988: 23–33; Emerton 1999: 323–34, n. 4.

[b] For the former, see Gropp 2001: 97–101 (Samaria, fourth century B.C.E.); Fales 1996 (Syria, seventh century); Dandamaev 1984b: 137–56 (Babylonia, seventh–fourth centuries). For the latter, see text no. 18 in this collection. In the fragmentary Samaria Papyrus 10 (fourth century) and possibly others from the same group, it appears that a slave was transferred to a creditor as an "antichretic" pledge. This term means that the creditor had the right to use the slave as income-earning property. Ordinarily this meant that the debtor did not have to pay interest.

[c] Both inscriptions are difficult to decipher, especially the second, in which some fragmentary lines (not all belonging to this text) overlap one another. Renz 1995: 3 passim reproduce drawings of fragments of the inscription by different scholars. The readings here, based on Renz 1995: 1:62–63, modified slightly on the basis of the drawings, are very uncertain.

[d] The lacuna is of uncertain length; the following words are written on a separate fragment.

[e] I have preserved the line numbers as they have appeared in several previous publications, but faint traces of the bottoms of the letters *m* and *r* can be made out in Meshel's photographs above "line 1." After line 8 there are several more apparently unrelated lines, three of them bearing portions of the alphabet, and one with the word "(the) grain" written twice.

[f] Or, less plausibly, reading *šmrn* as a participle with suffixed pronoun, "YHWH, our guardian" (Naveh 1979: 28).

[g] See the chapter introduction and Miller 2000: 29–43, 51–52 on the word.

[h] It is unclear whether *tmn* stands in the original or not. It is not visible in the published photographs and drawings. Some scholars claim to have read the word in the original. For details, see Renz 1995: 1:62. If the reading is correct, an alternative translation is "YHWH of the south." The Hebrew word means simply "south" and could in principle refer to Judah in distinction from Samaria. However, the word seems associated with a more specific southern place of theophany in Hab 3:3. An Edomite Teman is mentioned in Jer 49:7, 20; Ezek 25:13; Am 1:12; Obad 9.

[i] Possibly a scribal error for "Elimelek" (Ruth 1:2, 3, etc.), or "Elmalak" (Vattioni 1970: no. 11).

[j] Or perhaps, "the entire debt that I owe."

[k] Literally, "the debt that he borrows" (participle).

[l] The abbreviation *m'* is probably not to be read *maʿah* ("obolos, grain," a tiny coin of little value), as suggested by the editors of the *editio princeps* (Ephʿal and Naveh 1996: 90). A recently discovered Aramaic contract from seventh-century B.C.E. Syria similarly pledges a slave as collateral for a loan. The text contains the word *mina* written both in the abbreviated form *m'*, as here, and spelled out in full (Fales 1996). A *mina* was worth 60 shekels.

[m] Literally, "as we have seen."

[n] Literally, "the men."

Sources

Editions listed generally include translations, except for Rosenthal (Aramaic) and Davies (Hebrew). The sign # indicates the text number in editions conventionally cited in that manner, and references to Renz use his sigla. Otherwise page numbers are indicated. Under "Translations" are added only important translations published without the original text. Partial translations are listed only in a few cases of special importance. For more extensive bibliography, see, on the Aramaic letters, Porten (1968), Grelot (1972), Gibson (1975), Porten and Yardeni (1986, 1999), and Fitzmyer and Kaufman (1992) (also Whitehead 1974 [for nos. 37–48]); and, on the Hebrew texts, Pardee (1982) and Renz (1995). Pardee also has bibliography on the Phoenician letter.

1. **Editions:** Lidzbarski 1921: 5–15; Dupont-Sommer 1944–45: 24–61; Donner and Röllig 1966–69: #233; Gibson 1975: #20.
2. **Editions:** Dupont-Sommer 1948b: 43–68; Donner and Röllig 1966–69: #266; Fitzmyer 1965: 41–55; Gibson 1975: #21; Porten 1981: 36–52; Porten and Yardeni 1986: #1.1.
3. **Editions:** Bresciani and Kamil 1966: #1; Milik 1967: 581; Gibson 1975: #27.i; Porten and Yardeni 1986: #2.3.
   Translation: Grelot 1972: #25.
4. **Editions:** Bresciani and Kamil 1966: #3; Milik 1967: 582–83; Gibson 1975: #27.iii; Porten and Yardeni 1986: #2.4.
   Translation: Grelot 1972: #27.
5. **Editions:** Bresciani and Kamil 1966: #4; Milik 1967: 583; Gibson 1975: #27.iv; Porten and Yardeni 1986: #2.1.
   Translation: Grelot 1972: #28.
6. **Editions:** Bresciani and Kamil 1966: #2; Milik 1967: 581–82; Gibson 1975: #27.ii; Porten and Yardeni 1986: #2.2.
   Translation: Grelot 1972: #26.

7. **Editions:** Bresciani and Kamil 1966: #6; Milik 1967: 547–49; Gibson 1975: #27.vi; Porten and Yardeni 1986: #2.6.
   Translation: Grelot 1972: #30.
8. **Editions:** Bresciani and Kamil 1966: #5; Milik 1967: 583–84; Gibson 1975: #27.v; Porten and Yardeni 1986: #2.5.
   Translation: Grelot 1972: #29.
9. **Editions:** Bresciani and Kamil 1966: #7; Milik 1967: 584; Gibson 1975: #27.vii; Porten and Yardeni 1986: #2.7.
   Translation: Grelot 1972: #31.
10. **Editions:** Bresciani 1960: 11–24; Fitzmyer 1962: 15–22; Gibson 1975: #28; Porten and Yardeni 1986: #3.3
    Translation: Grelot 1972: #14.
11. **Editions:** Bresciani 1960: 11–24; Fitzmyer 1962: 22–23; Porten and Yardeni 1986: #3.4.
11a. **Editions:** Naveh and Shaked 1971; Porten and Yardeni 1986: #3.10.
    Translation: Grelot 1972: #109.
12. **Editions:** *CIS* ii: #137; Sachau 1911: #78/3; Dupont-Sommer 1948a: 117–30; Levine 1964: 18–22; Donner and Röllig 1966–69: #270; Gibson 1975: #123; Porten and Yardeni 1999: #7.17.
    Translations: Porten 1968: 275; Grelot 1972: #21.
13. **Editions:** Sayce 1909: 154–55; *RES:* #1295; Lidzbarski 1909–15: 119–21; Porten and Yardeni 1999: #7.29.
    Translations: Porten 1968: 179; Grelot 1972: #92.
14. **Editions:** Dupont-Sommer 1963: 53–58; Porten and Yardeni 1999: #7.10.
    Translations: Grelot 1972: #99.
15. **Editions:** Sachau 1911: #76/1; Greenfield 1960: 98–102; Porten and Yardeni 1999: #7.8.
    Translations: Porten 1968: 87, 132; Grelot 1972: #95.
16. Same as no. 15.
17. **Editions:** Cowley 1929: 107–11; Porten and Yardeni 1999: #7.1.
    Translations: Grelot 1972: #23.
18. **Editions:** Sayce and Cowley 1906: "M"; Lidzbarski 1903–7: 236–38; *RES:* #492, #1800; Porten and Yardeni 1999: #7.9.
    Translations: Porten 1968: 204; Grelot 1972: #22.
19. **Editions:** Sayce 1911: 183–84; *RES:* #1793; Dupont-Sommer 1946–47a: 46–51; Porten and Yardeni 1999: #7.6.
    Translations: Porten 1968: 131, 276; Grelot 1972: #94.
20. **Editions:** Dupont-Sommer 1945: 17–28; Porten and Yardeni 1999: #7.21.
    Translations: Porten 1968: 275; Ginsberg 1969: 491; Grelot 1972: #87.
21. **Editions:** Aimé-Giron 1926: 27–29; Dupont-Sommer 1946–47b: 79–87; Porten and Yardeni 1999: #7.18.
    Translations: Porten 1968: 277; Grelot 1972: #90.

22. **Editions:** Dupont-Sommer 1949: 29–39; Rosenthal 1967: #II.A.5; Porten and Yardeni 1999: #7.16.
    Translation: Grelot 1972: #91.

23. **Editions:** Dupont-Sommer 1948a: 109–16; Porten and Yardeni 1999: #7.7.
    Translation: Porten 1968: 90, 277.

24. **Editions:** Dupont-Sommer 1942–45: 65–75; Porten and Yardeni 1999: #7.2.
    Translations: Porten 1968: 276; Grelot 1972: #19.

25. **Editions:** Lozachmeur 1971: 81–93; Porten and Yardeni 1999: #7.5.

25a. **Editions:** Lozachmeur 1990; Porten and Yardeni 1999: #7.44.

26. **Editions:** Dupont-Sommer 1957: 403–9; Porten and Yardeni 1999: #7.35.

27. **Editions:** Aimé-Giron 1931: 6–7; Lidzbarski 1909–15: 121–22; *RES:* #1296; Porten and Yardeni 1999: #7.45.
    Translation: Grelot 1972: #20.

27a. **Editions:** Dupont-Sommer 1944; Porten and Yardeni 1999: #7.30.
    Translations: Porten 1968: 159; Ginsberg 1969: 491; Grelot 1972: #88.

28. **Editions:** Porten and Yardeni 1991: 207–17; 1999: #7.20.

29. Same as no. 28.

30. **Editions:** Sachau 1911: #6; Cowley 1923: #21; Porten and Yardeni 1986: #4.1.
    Translation: Grelot 1972: #96.

31. **Editions:** Sachau 1911: #11; Cowley 1923: #38; Porten and Yardeni 1986: #4.3
    Translation: Grelot 1972: #98.

32. **Editions:** Sachau 1911: ##43 + 33; Cowley 1923: ##56 + 34; Porten and Yardeni 1986: #4.4.
    Translation: Grelot 1972: #100.

33. **Editions:** Euting 1903: 297–311; Cowley 1923: #27; Porten and Yardeni 1986: #4.5.
    Translation: Grelot 1972: #101.

34. **Editions:** Sachau 1911: ##1–2; Cowley 1923: ##30–31; Rosenthal 1967: #II.A.1; Porten and Yardeni 1986: ##4.7–4.8.
    Translations: Ginsberg 1969: 491–92; Grelot 1972: #102.

35. **Editions:** Sachau 1911: #3; Cowley 1923: #32; Porten and Yardeni 1986: #4.9.
    Translations: Ginsberg 1969: 492; Grelot 1972: #103.

36. **Editions:** Sachau 1911: #5; Cowley 1923: #33; Porten and Yardeni 1986: #4.10.
    Translations: Ginsberg 1969: 492; Grelot 1972: #104.

37. **Editions:** Driver 1954, 1965: #2; Whitehead 1974: 38–42; Porten and Yardeni 1986: #6.4.
    Translation: Grelot 1972: #62.

38. **Editions:** Driver 1954, 1965: #4; Whitehead 1974: 48–53; Porten and Yardeni 1986: #6.8.
    Translation: Grelot 1972: #65.
39. **Editions:** Driver 1954, 1965: #3; Whitehead 1974: 42–48; Porten and Yardeni 1986: #6.3.
    Translation: Grelot 1972: #64.
40. **Editions:** Driver 1954, 1965: #5; Whitehead 1974: 53–59; Rosenthal 1967: #II.A.2; Porten and Yardeni 1986: #6.7.
    Translation: Grelot 1972: #66.
41. **Editions:** Driver 1954, 1965: #6; Whitehead 1974: 59–68; Porten and Yardeni 1986: #6.9.
    Translation: Grelot 1972: #67.
42. **Editions:** Driver 1954, 1965: #8; Rosenthal 1967: #II.A.3; Whitehead 1974: 77–84; Porten and Yardeni 1986: #6.11.
    Translation: Grelot 1972: #69.
43. **Editions:** Driver 1954, 1965: #7; Whitehead 1974: 69–76; Porten and Yardeni 1986: #6.10.
    Translation: Grelot 1972: #68.
44. **Editions:** Driver 1954, 1965: #10; Whitehead 1974: 90–94; Porten and Yardeni 1986: #6.13.
    Translation: Grelot 1972: #71.
45. **Editions:** Driver 1954, 1965: #11; Whitehead 1974: 94–99; Porten and Yardeni 1986: #6.14.
    Translation: Grelot 1972: #72.
46. **Editions:** Driver 1954, 1965: #9; Rosenthal 1967: #II.A.4; Whitehead 1974: 84–89; Porten and Yardeni 1986: #6.12.
    Translation: Grelot 1972: #70.
47. **Editions:** Driver 1954, 1965: #12; Whitehead 1974: 99–108; Porten and Yardeni 1986: #6.15.
    Translation: Grelot 1972: #73.
48. **Editions:** Driver 1954, 1965: #13; Whitehead 1974: 108–12; Porten and Yardeni 1986: #6.16.
    Translation: Grelot 1972: #74.
49. **Editions:** Sachau 1911: #8; Cowley 1923: #26; Porten and Yardeni 1986: #6.2.
    Translation: Grelot 1972: #61.
50. **Editions:** Naveh 1960; Gibson 1971: 26–30; Pardee 1982: #1; Davies 1991: #7.001; Renz 1995: MHas(7):1; Gogel 1998: 6.1.16 Meṣad Ḥashavyahu 1.
    Translations: Albright 1969: 568; Lemaire 1977: 259–68.
50a. **Editions:** Bordreuil, Israel, and Pardee 1996, 1998; Gogel 1998: 6.1.17 Moussaïeff Ostracon 2.
    Translation: Shanks 1997.

50b. **Editions:** Bordreuil, Israel, and Pardee 1996, 1998; Gogel 1998: 6.1.17 Moussaïeff Ostracon 1.
   Translation: Shanks 1997.

51. **Editions:** Aharoni 1975, 1981: #40; Pardee 1982: #22; Davies 1991: #2.040; Renz 1995: Arad(8):40; Gogel 1998: 6.1.1 Arad 40.
   Translation: Lemaire 1977: 207–9.

52. **Editions:** Aharoni 1975, 1981: #88; Davies 1991: #2.088; Renz 1995: Arad(7):88; Gogel 1998: 6.1.1 Arad 88.
   Translation: Lemaire 1977: 220–21.

53. **Editions:** Aharoni 1975, 1981: #24; Pardee 1982: #20; Davies 1991: #2.024; Renz 1995: Arad(6):24; Gogel 1998: 6.1.1 Arad 24.
   Translation: Lemaire 1977: 188–95.

54. **Editions:** Aharoni 1975, 1981: #21; Pardee 1982: #19; Davies 1991: #2.021; Renz 1995: Arad(6):21; Gogel 1998: 6.1.1 Arad 21.
   Translation: Lemaire 1977: 186–87.

55. **Editions:** Aharoni 1975, 1981: #18; Pardee 1982: #18; Davies 1991: #2.018; Renz 1995: Arad(6):18; Gogel 1998: 6.1.1 Arad 18.
   Translation: Lemaire 1977: 179–84; Albright 1969: 569.

56. **Editions:** Aharoni 1975, 1981: #1; Pardee 1982: #2; Davies 1991: #2.001; Renz 1995: Arad(6):1; Gogel 1998: 6.1.1 Arad 1.
   Translation: Lemaire 1977: 155–61.

57. **Editions:** Aharoni 1975, 1981: #2; Pardee 1982: #3; Davies 1991: #2.002; Renz 1995: Arad(6):2; Gogel 1998: 6.1.1 Arad 2.
   Translations: Lemaire 1977: 161–63.

58. **Editions:** Aharoni 1975, 1981: #3; Pardee 1982: #4; Davies 1991: #2.003; Renz 1995: Arad(6):3; Gogel 1998: 6.1.1 Arad 3.
   Translation: Lemaire 1977: 163–66.

59. **Editions:** Aharoni 1975, 1981: #17; Pardee 1982: #17; Davies 1991: #2.017; Renz 1995: Arad(6):17; Gogel 1998: 6.1.1 Arad 17.
   Translation: Lemaire 1977: 174–79.

60. **Editions:** Aharoni 1975, 1981: #16; Pardee 1982: #16; Davies 1991: #2.016; Renz 1995: Arad(6):16; Gogel 1998: 6.1.1 Arad 16.
   Translation: Lemaire 1977: 172–74.

61. **Editions:** Torczyner 1938: #2; Diringer 1953: #2; Pardee 1982: #24; Davies 1991: #1.002; Renz 1995: Lak(6):1.2; Gogel 1998: 6.1.15 Lachish 2.
   Translations: Albright 1969: 322; Lemaire 1977: 97–100.

62. **Editions:** Torczyner 1938: #3; Diringer 1953: #3; Pardee 1982: #25; Cross 1985; Davies 1991: #1.003; Renz 1995: Lak(6):1.3; Gogel 1998: 6.1.15 Lachish 3.
   Translations: Albright 1969: 322; Lemaire 1977: 100–109.

63. **Editions:** Torczyner 1938: #4; Diringer 1953: #4; Pardee 1982: #26; Davies 1991: #1.004; Renz 1995: Lak(6):1.4; Gogel 1998: 6.1.15 Lachish 4.
   Translations: Albright 1969: 322; Lemaire 1977: 110–17.

64. **Editions:** Torczyner 1938: #6; Diringer 1953: #6; Pardee 1982: #28; Davies 1991: #1.006.; Renz 1995: Lak(6):1.6; Gogel 1998: 6.1.15 Lachish 6.
    Translations: Albright 1969: 322; Lemaire 1977: 120–24.
65. **Editions:** Torczyner 1938: #16; Diringer 1953: #16; Pardee 1982: #33; Davies 1991: #1.016; Renz 1995: Lak(6):1.16; Gogel 1998: 6.1.15 Lachish 16.
    Translations: Lemaire 1977: 131.
66. **Editions:** Torczyner 1938: #5; Diringer 1953: #5; Pardee 1982: #27; Davies 1991: #1.005; Renz 1995: Lak(6):1.5; Gogel 1998: 6.1.15 Lachish 5.
    Translations: Albright 1969: 322; Lemaire 1977: 117–20.
67. **Editions:** Torczyner 1938: #9; Diringer 1953: #9; Pardee 1982: #30; Davies 1991: #1.009; Renz 1995: Lak(6):1.9; Gogel 1998: 6.1.15 Lachish 9.
    Translations: Albright 1969: 322; Lemaire 1977: 127–28.
67a. **Editions:** Meshel 1978: ("First and Second Pithoi"); Lemaire 1984; Dever 1984; Renz 1995: KAgr(9):8–9; Gogel 1998: 6.1.14 Kuntillet ʿAjrûd 14–15.
67b. **Editions:** Milik 1961: #17; Pardee 1982: #36; Davies 1991: #33.001; Renz 1995: Mur(7):1; Gogel 1998: 6.1.18 Murabaʿat papMur 17a.
68. **Edition:** Beit Arieh and Cresson 1985.
69. **Editions:** Yassine and Teixidor 1986; Aufrecht 1989: 334–37.
70. **Editions:** Aimé-Giron 1941; Donner and Röllig 1966–69: #50; Pardee 1982: 165–68.
71. **Edition:** Ephʿal and Naveh 1996: #199.
72. **Edition:** Ephʿal and Naveh 1996: #196.

Concordance of Texts

CHAPTER I. Aramaic Diplomatic-Military Correspondence

1. **Ashur Ostracon** "Report of an Assyrian Officer"
    Museum Designation: Berlin, St. Mus. VA 8384
    CAL: AssOstr
    KAI: 233
2. **Adon Papyrus** "Appeal to Pharaoh for Military Aid"
    Museum Designation: Cairo, Eg. Mus. J. 86984 = 3483
    TADA: 1.1ᵃ
    KAI: 266

CHAPTER II. Business and Family Letters

3. **Hermopolis 1**
    Museum Designation: Cairo Univ., Arch. Mus. P. 1687
    DAE: 25
    TADA: 2.3
4. **Hermopolis 3**
    Museum Designation: Cairo Univ., Arch. Mus. P. 1689
    DAE: 27
    TADA: 2.4
5. **Hermopolis 4**
    Museum Designation: Cairo Univ., Arch. Mus. P. 1690
    DAE: 28
    TADA: 2.1
6. **Hermopolis 2**
    Museum Designation: Cairo Univ., Arch. Mus. P. 1688
    DAE: 26
    TADA: 2.2
7. **Hermopolis 6**
    Museum Designation: Cairo Univ., Arch. Mus. P. 1692

	DAE:	30
	TADA:	2.6
8.	**Hermopolis 5**	
	Museum Designation:	Cairo Univ., Arch. Mus. P. 1691
	DAE:	29
	TADA:	2.5
9.	**Hermopolis 7**	
	Museum Designation:	Cairo Univ., Arch. Mus. P. 1693
	DAE:	31
	TADA:	2.7
10.	**Padua 1**	"To a Son on a Journey"
	Museum Designation:	Museo Civico di Padova Aram. Pap. 1
	DAE:	14
	TADA:	3.3
11.	**Padua 2**	"A Son to His Mother"
	Museum Designation:	Museo Civico di Padova Aram. Pap. 1
	TADA:	3.4
11a.	**Berlin Papyrus 23000**	"Grain Shipments"
	DAE:	109 •
	TADA:	3.10

CHAPTER III. Ostraca from Elephantine

12.	**Berlin, St. Mus. 1137**	"A Dream and Family Matters"
	DAE:	21
	TADD:	7.17
13.	**O. Cairo 35468a**	"Money for a Religious Society"
	DAE:	92
	TADD:	7.29
14.	**O. Clermont-Ganneau 44**	"A Report of Imprisonment"
	DAE:	99
	TADD:	7.10 '
15.	**Berlin, St. Mus. 11383**	"Sheepshearing"
	DAE:	95
	TADD:	7.8 (concave)
16.	**Berlin, St. Mus. 11383**	"Bread and Flour"
	DAE:	95
	TADD:	7.8 (convex)
17.	**Cambridge 131–133**	"Sheep Marketing"
	DAE:	23
	TADD:	7.1
18.	**Bodleian** (Ashmolean)	
	Aram. Inscr. 1 (Lost)	"Money and Slaves"
	DAE:	22

	TADD:	7.9
19.	**Bodleian** (Ashmolean)	
	Aram. Inscr. 7	"Family Messages: Passover"
	DAE:	94
	TADD:	7.6
20.	**O. Clermont-Ganneau 70**	"Repair of a Garment"
	DAE:	87
	TADD:	7.21
21.	**O. Cairo 49624**	"Dedication of a Tunic"
	DAE:	90
	TADD:	7.18
22.	**O. Clermont-Ganneau 152**	"Handling of Produce and the Sabbath"
	DAE:	91
	TADD:	7.16
23.	**O. Clermont-Ganneau 16**	"Shopping Lists and Shipping Orders-A"
	TADD:	7.7
24.	**O. Clermont-Ganneau 169**	"Shopping Lists and Shipping Orders-B"
	DAE:	19
	TADD:	7.2
25.	**O. Clermont-Ganneau 228**	"Shopping Lists and Shipping Orders-C"
	TADD:	7.5
25a.	**O. Clermont-Ganneau 125?**	"Shopping Lists and Shipping Orders-D"
	TADD:	7.44
26.	**O. Clermont-Ganneau 186**	"Shopping Lists and Shipping Orders-E"
	TADD:	7.35
27.	**O. Cairo 35468b**	"Shopping Lists and Shipping Orders-F"
	RES:	1296
	DAE:	20
	TADD:	7.45
27a.	**O. Clermont-Ganneau 277**	"Greetings in the Names of the Gods"
	DAE:	88
	TADD:	7.30
28.	**BM 45035a**	("Miscellaneous-A")
	TADD:	7.20 (concave)
29.	**BM 45035b**	("Miscellaneous-B")
	TADD:	7.20 (convex)

CHAPTER IV. Archives of the Jewish Community at Elephantine

30.	**AP 21**	"Passover (?) and Unleavened Bread"
	Museum Designation:	Berlin, St. Mus. P. 13464
	DAE:	96
	TADA:	4.1
31.	**AP 38**	"An Accusation and a Warning"

	Museum Designation:	Cairo P. 3435 = J. 43472
	DAE:	98
	TADA:	4.3
32.	**AP 56+34**	"Riot and Imprisonment"
	Museum Designation:	Berlin, St. Mus. P. 13456 = Cairo P. 3439 = J. 43476)
	DAE:	100
	TADA:	4.4
33.	**AP 27**	"Accusation of Stopping a Well"
	Museum Designation:	U. of Strasbourg Library, P. Aram. 2
	DAE:	101
	TADA:	4.5
34.	**AP 30/31**	"Razing of Temple and Petition for Aid"
	Museum Designation:	Berlin, St. Mus. P. 13495/Cairo P. 3428 = J. 43465
	DAE:	102
	TADA:	4.7 and 4.8
35.	**AP 32**	"Memorandum on Reconstructing the Temple"
	Museum Designation:	Berlin, St. Mus. P. 13497
	DAE:	103
	TADA:	4.9
36.	**AP 33**	"A Petition and a Bribe"
	Museum Designation:	Cairo P. 3430 = J. 43467
	DAE:	104
	TADA:	4.10

CHAPTER V. Letters from Persian Officials

37.	**AD 2**	"Appointment of a Steward"
	Museum Designation:	Bodleian Pell. Aram. XII
	DAE:	62
	TADA:	6.4
38.	**AD 4**	"Reprimand to an Insubordinate Officer"
	Museum Designation:	Bodleian Pell. Aram. II
	DAE:	65
	TADA:	6.8
39.	**AD 3**	"Slaves-A"
	Museum Designation:	Bodleian Pell. Aram. VII + Frag. 7.1
	DAE:	64
	TADA:	6.3
40.	**AD 5**	"Slaves-B"
	Museum Designation:	Bodleian Pell. Aram. IV

CHAPTER VI. Two Hebrew Petitions and a Royal Order

Museum Designation: IM 60–67
HAHL: 1
Renz:[b] MHas(7):1
50a. **Petition of a Widow**
Collection: Moussaïeff Hebrew Ostracon #2
50b. **A Royal Order concerning Silver for the Temple**
Collection: Moussaïeff Hebrew Ostracon #1

CHAPTER VII. Judean Military-Administrative Letters from Arad and Lachish

51. **Arad 40** "A Report from Edom"
Museum Designation: IM 67–631
HAHL: 22
Renz: Arad (8):40
52. **Arad 88** "A Royal Fragment"
Museum Designation: Arad Excav. Reg. No. 7904/1
Renz: Arad (7):88
53. **Arad 24** "Orders from the King"
Museum Designation: IM 72–121
HAHL: 20
Renz: Arad (6):24
54. **Arad 21** "Fragmentary Letter"
Museum Designation: IM 72–126
HAHL: 19
Renz: Arad (6):21
55. **Arad 18** "Rations and Other Matters-A"
Museum Designation: IM 67–669
HAHL: 18
Renz: Arad (6):18
56. **Arad 1** "Rations and Other Matters-B"
Museum Designation: IM 67–713
HAHL: 2
Renz: Arad (6):1
57. **Arad 2** "Rations and Other Matters-C"
Museum Designation: IM 67–625
HAHL: 3
Renz: Arad (6):2
58. **Arad 3** "Rations and Other Matters-D"
Museum Designation: IM 67–623
HAHL: 4
Renz: Arad (6):3
59. **Arad 17** "Rations and Other Matters-E"
Museum Designation: IM 67–624

	HAHL:	17
	Renz:	Arad (6):17
60.	**Arad 16**	"Rations and Other Matters-F"
	Museum Designation:	IM 67–990
	HAHL:	16
	Renz:	Arad (6):16
61.	**Lachish 2**	"Greetings to a Superior Officer"
	Museum Designation:	BM 125 702
	HAHL:	24
	Renz:	Lak (6):1.2
62.	**Lachish 3**	"Protest of Literacy, Troop Movements, etc."
	Museum Designation:	IM 38–127
	HAHL:	25
	Renz:	Lak (6):1.3
63.	**Lachish 4**	"Report on Signal-Fire and Other Matters"
	Museum Designation:	IM 38–128
	HAHL:	26
	Renz:	Lak (6):1.4
64.	**Lachish 6**	"Morale"
	Museum Designation:	IM 38-129
	HAHL:	28
	Renz:	Lak (6):1.6
65.	**Lachish 16**	"Fragment Mentioning a Prophet"
	Museum Designation:	BM 125 706
	HAHL:	33
	Renz:	Lak (6):1.16
66.	**Lachish 5**	"Rations-A"
	Museum Designation:	BM 125 703
	HAHL:	27
	Renz:	Lak (6):1.5
67.	**Lachish 9**	"Rations-B"
	Museum Designation:	BM 125 705
	HAHL:	30
	Renz:	Lak (6):1.9

CHAPTER VIII. Fragmentary and Miscellaneous

67a. **Epistolary Formulas from Kuntillet ʿAjrûd**
Renz: KAgr (9):8–9

67b. **A Papyrus Letter Fragment from Murabaʿat**
DJD: 2, 17a
Renz: Mur (7):1

Notes

[a] *TADA* and *TADD* numbers correspond to *CAL* designations.

[b] References to Renz in the concordance are to Renz 1995.

Bibliography

Académie des Inscriptions et Belles Lettres
1889 *Corpus inscriptionum semiticarum.* Part 2, vol. 1. Paris: Imprimerie Nationale.
1900–68 *Répertoire d'épigraphie sémitique.* Paris: Imprimerie Nationale.

Aharoni, Yohanan
1975 *Arad Inscriptions* [Hebrew]. Jerusalem: Israel Exploration Society.
1981 *Arad Inscriptions.* Translated by Judith Ben-Or. Edited and revised by Anson F. Rainey. Jerusalem: Israel Exploration Society.

[Aimé-]Giron, Noël
1926 "Trois ostraca araméens d'Éléphantine." *ASAE* 26:27–29.
1931 *Textes araméens d'Égypte.* Cairo: Service des Antiquités de l'Égypte.
1941 "Adversaria semitica (III): VIII, Baal Saphon et les dieux de Tahpanhès dans un nouveau papyrus phénicien." *ASAE* 40:433–60.

Albright, William F.
1969 "Palestinian Inscriptions." Pages 320–22, 568–69 in *Ancient Near Eastern Texts Relating to the Old Testament.* Edited by J. B. Pritchard. 3d ed. Princeton: Princeton University Press.

Aufrecht, Walter E.
1989 *A Corpus of Ammonite Inscriptions.* Ancient Near Eastern Texts and Studies 4. Lewiston, N.Y.: Edwin Mellen.

Baly, Denis
1984 "The Geography of Palestine and the Levant in Relation to Its History." Pages 1–24 in *Introduction; The Persian Period.* Edited by W. D. Davies and Louis Finkelstein. Vol. 1 of *The*

Cambridge History of Judaism. Cambridge: Cambridge University Press.

Begin, Ze'ev B., and Avihu Grushka
1999   "Where Was Lachish 4 Written?" [Hebrew]. *Eretz Israel* 26: 13–24 [Eng. summary, pp. 226*–27*].

Beit-Arieh, Itzhaq, and Bruce Cresson
1985   "An Edomite Ostracon from Horvat Uza." *Tel Aviv* 12:96–101.

Benoit, P., J. T. Milik, and Roland de Vaux
1961   *Les grottes de Murabbaʿât.* DJD 2. Oxford: Clarendon.

Benz, Frank L.
1972   *Personal Names in the Phoenician and Punic Inscriptions.* Studia Pohl 6. Rome: Biblical Institute Press.

Bivar, A. D. H.
1985   "Achaemenid Coins, Weights and Measures." Pages 610–39 in *The Median and Achaemenian Periods.* Edited by Ilya Gershevitch. Vol. 2 of *The Cambridge History of Iran.* Cambridge: Cambridge University Press.

Boardman, John
1988a   "The Greek World." Pages 95–178 in *Persia, Greece and the Western Mediterranean, c. 525–479 B.C.* [plates]. Edited by John Boardman. Supplement to vol. 4 of *The Cambridge Ancient History.* Cambridge: Cambridge University Press.

Boardman, John, ed.
1988b   *Persia, Greece and the Western Mediterranean, c. 525–479 B.C.* Vol. 4 of *The Cambridge Ancient History.* Cambridge: Cambridge University Press.

1988c   *Persia, Greece and the Western Mediterranean, c. 525–479 B.C.* [plates]. Supplement to vol. 4 of *The Cambridge Ancient History 4.* Cambridge: Cambridge University Press.

Bordreuil, Pierre, Felice Israel, and Dennis Pardee
1996   "Deux ostraca paléo-hébreux de la collection Sh. Moussaïeff: I) Contribution financière obligatoire pour le temple de YHWH, II) Réclamation d'une veuve auprès d'un fonctionnaire." *Semitica* 46:49–76 + pls. 7–8.

1998   "King's Command and Widow's Plea." *Near Eastern Archaeology* 61:2–13.

Brandenstein, Wilhelm, and Manfred Mayrhofer
1964   *Handbuch des Altpersischen.* Wiesbaden: Harrassowitz.

Bresciani, Edda
1960   "Papiri aramaici egiziani di epoca persiana presso il Museo Civico di Padova." *Rivista degli studi orientali* 35:11–24.

1984   "The Diaspora: C. Egypt, Persian Satrapy." Pages 358–72 in *Introduction; The Persian Period.* Edited by W. D. Davies and Louis Finkelstein. Vol. 1 of *The Cambridge History of Judaism*. Cambridge: Cambridge University Press.

1985　"The Persian Occupation of Egypt." Pages 502–28 in *The Median and Achaemenian Periods*. Edited by Ilya Gershevitch. Vol. 2 of *The Cambridge History of Iran*. Cambridge: Cambridge University Press.

Bresciani, Edda, and Murad Kamil

1966　"Le lettere aramaiche di Hermopoli." Pages 356–428 in *Atti della Accademia Nazionale dei Lincei*. Classe di Scienze morali, storiche e filologiche, 8/12. Rome: Accademia nazionale dei Lincei.

Briant, Pierre

1996　"Une curieuse affaire à Éléphantine en 410 av. n.è.: Widranga, le sanctuaire de Khnûm et le temple de Yahweh." *Méditerranées* 6/7:115–35.

Bright, John

1981　*A History of Israel*. 3d ed. Philadelphia: Westminster.

Burn, A. R.

1985　"Persia and the Greeks." Pages 292–391 in *The Median and Achaemenian Periods*. Edited by Ilya Gershevitch. Vol. 2 of *The Cambridge History of Iran*. Cambridge: Cambridge University Press.

Coats, George

1970　"Self Abasement and Insult Formulas." *JBL* 89:14–26.

Cogan, Mordechai, and Hayim Tadmor

1988　*II Kings*. Anchor Bible 11. Garden City, N.Y.: Doubleday.

Cook, J. M.

1983　*The Persian Empire*. London: J. M. Dent & Sons.

1985　"The Rise of the Achaemenids and Establishment of Their Empire." Pages 200–291 in *The Median and Achaemenian Periods*. Edited by Ilya Gershevitch. Vol. 2 of *The Cambridge History of Iran*. Cambridge: Cambridge University Press.

Cowley, A. E.

1923　*Aramaic Papyri of the Fifth Century B.C.* Oxford: Clarendon.

1929　"Two Aramaic Ostraca." *Journal of the Royal Asiatic Society* 107–12.

Cross, Frank Moore

1985　"A Literate Soldier: Lachish Letter III." Pages 41–47 in *Biblical and Related Studies Presented to Samuel Iwry*. Edited by Ann Kort and Scott Morschauser. Winona Lake, Ind.: Eisenbrauns.

Dalman, Gustaf H.

1938　*Aramäisch-Neuhebräisches Handwörterbuch zu Targum, Talmud und Midrasch*. Hildesheim: Olms.

Dandamaev, Muhammad A.
1984a "The Diaspora: A. Babylonia in the Persian Age." Pages 326–42 in *Introduction; The Persian Period*. Edited by W. D. Davies and Louis Finkelstein. Vol. 1 of *The Cambridge History of Judaism*. Cambridge: Cambridge University Press.
1984b *Slavery in Babylonia: From Nabopolassar to Alexander the Great (626–331 BC)*. Translated by Victoria Powell. Edited by Marvin A. Powell and B. David Weisberg. DeKalb: Northern Illinois University.

Dandamaev, Muhammad A., and Vladimir Lukonin
1989 *The Culture and Social Institutions of Ancient Iran*. Edited and translated by Philip L. Kohl and D. J. Dadson. Cambridge: Cambridge University Press.

Davies, G. I.
1991 *Ancient Hebrew Inscriptions*. Assisted by M. N. A. Bockmuehl, D. de Lacey, and A. J. Poulter. Cambridge: Cambridge University Press.

Davies, W. D., and Louis Finkelstein, eds.
1984 *Introduction; The Persian Period*. Vol. 1 of *The Cambridge History of Judaism*. Cambridge: Cambridge University Press.

Dever, William G.
1984 "Asherah, Consort of Yahweh? New Evidence from Kuntillet ʿAjrûd." *BASOR* 255:21–37.
1985 "Weights and Measures." Pages 1126–31 in *Harper's Bible Dictionary*. Edited by Paul J. Achtemeier et al. San Francisco: Harper & Row.

Dietrich, Manfried
1970 *Die Aramäer Südbabyloniens in der Sargonidenzeit*. Alter Orient und altes Testament 7. Neukirchen-Vluyn: Butzon & Bercker Kevelaer.

Dion, Paul-Eugène
1997 *Les Araméens à l'Âge Du Fer: Histoire Politique et Structures Sociales*. Etudes bibliques NS 34. Paris: Gabalda.

Diringer, David
1953 "Early Hebrew Inscriptions." Pages 331–59 in *The Iron Age*. Edited by Olga Tufnell et al. Lachish 3. London: Oxford University Press.

Donner, Herbert, and Wolfgang Röllig
1966–69 *Kanaanäische und Aramäische Inschriften*. 2d ed. Wiesbaden: Harrassowitz.

Driver, Godfrey R.
1954 *Aramaic Documents of the Fifth Century B.C.* Oxford: Clarendon.

1965   *Aramaic Documents of the Fifth Century B.C.* Oxford: Clarendon.

Dupont-Sommer, André
1942–45 "Un ostracon araméen inédit d'Éléphantine adressé à Ahutab." *Revue des études sémitiques* n.v.:65–75.
1944   " 'Bêl et Nabû, Šamaš et Nergal' sur un ostracon araméen inédit d'Éléphantine." *Revue de l'histoire des religions* 128:28–39.
1944–45 "L'ostracon araméen d'Assour." *Syria* 24:24–61.
1945   "Le syncretisme religieux des juifs d'Éléphantine d'après un ostracon araméen inédit." *Revue de l'histoire des religions* 130:17–28.
1946–47a "Sur la fête de la Pâque dans les documents araméens d'Éléphantine." *Revue des études juives* 107:39–51.
1946–47b "Maison de Yahvé et vêtements sacrés à Éléphantine." *Journal asiatique* 235:79–87.
1948a   "Ostraca araméens d'Éléphantine." *ASAE* 48:109–30.
1948b   "Un papyrus araméen d'époque saïte découverte à Saqqarah." *Semitica* 1:43–68.
1949   "L'ostracon araméen du sabbat." *Semitica* 2:29–39.
1957   "Un ostracon araméen inédit d'Éléphantine." *Rivista degli studi orientali* 32:403–9.
1963   "Un ostracon araméen inédit d'Éléphantine (collection Clermont-Ganneau No 44)." Pages 53–58 in *Hebrew and Semitic Studies Presented to Godfrey Rolles Driver.* Edited by D. Winton Thomas and W. D. McHardy. Oxford: Clarendon.

Emerton, John A.
1999   " 'Yahweh and His Asherah:' The Goddess or Her Symbol?" *Vetus Testamentum* 49:315–37.

Eph'al, Israel, and Joseph Naveh
1996   *Aramaic Ostraca of the Fourth Century BC from Idumaea.* Jerusalem: Magnes (Israel Exploration Society).
1998   "Remarks on the Recently Published Moussaieff Ostraca." *IEJ* 48:269–73.

Euting, J.
1903   "Notice sur un papyrus égypto-araméen de la Bibliothèque Impériale de Strasbourg." *Mémoires presentées par divers savants à l'Académie des Inscriptions et Belles-Lettres* 11:297–311.

Fales, Frederick Mario
1987   "Aramaic Letters and Neo-Assyrian Letters: Philological and Methodological Notes." *JAOS* 107:451–69.
1996   "An Aramaic Tablet from Tell Shioukh Fawkani, Syria." *Semitica* 46:81–121.

Fitzmyer, Joseph A.
> 1962   "The Padua Aramaic Papyrus Letters." *JNES* 21:15–24.
> 1965   "The Aramaic Letter of King Adon to the Egyptian Pharaoh." *Biblica* 46:41–55.
> 1979   "The Phases of the Aramaic Language." Pages 57–84 in *A Wandering Aramean: Collected Aramaic Essays.* Society of Biblical Literature Monograph Series 25. Missoula, Mont.: Scholars Press.
> 1981   "Aramaic Epistolography." *Semeia* 22:25–56.

Fitzmyer, Joseph A., and Stephen Kaufman
> 1992   *Old, Official, and Biblical Aramaic.* Vol. 1 of *An Aramaic Bibliography.* Baltimore: Johns Hopkins University Press.

Frye, Richard N.
> 1984   *The History of Ancient Iran.* Handbuch der Altertumswissenschaft. Munich: C. H. Beck.

Gershevitch, Ilya, ed.
> 1985   *The Median and Achaemenian Periods.* Vol. 2 of *The Cambridge History of Iran.* Cambridge: Cambridge University Press.

Gibson, John C. L.
> 1971   *Hebrew and Moabite Inscriptions.* Vol. 1 of *Textbook of Syrian Semitic Inscriptions.* Oxford: Clarendon.
> 1975   *Aramaic Inscriptions.* Vol. 2 of *Textbook of Syrian Semitic Inscriptions.* Oxford: Clarendon.

Ginsberg, H. L.
> 1969   "Letters of the Jews of Elephantine." Pages 491–92 in *Ancient Near Eastern Texts Relating to the Old Testament.* Edited by J. B. Pritchard. 3d ed. Princeton: Princeton University Press.

Gogel, Sandra Landis
> 1998   *A Grammar of Epigraphic Hebrew.* Society of Biblical Literature Resources for Biblical Study 23. Atlanta: Scholars Press.

Greenfield, Jonas C.
> 1960   "Le bain des brebis." *Orientalia* 29:98–102.
> 1985   "Aramaic in the Achaemenian Empire." Pages 698–713 in *The Median and Achaemenian Periods.* Edited by Ilya Gershevitch. Vol. 2 of *The Cambridge History of Iran.* Cambridge: Cambridge University Press.

Grelot, Pierre
> 1972   *Documents araméens d'Égypte.* Paris: Cerf.

Gropp, Douglas M.
> 2001   *Wadi Daliyeh II: The Samaria Papyri from Wadi Daliyeh.* DJD 28. Oxford: Clarendon.

Hallock, R. T.
1985   "The Evidence of the Persepolis Tablets." Pages 588–609 in *The Median and Achaemenian Periods*. Edited by Ilya Gershevitch. Vol. 2 of *The Cambridge History of Iran*. Cambridge: Cambridge University Press.

Hayes, John H., and James Maxwell Miller, eds.
1977   *Israelite and Judean History*. Philadelphia: Westminster.

Hillers, Delbert R.
1979   "Redemption in Letters 6 and 2 from Hermopolis." *Ugarit-Forschungen* 11:379–82.

Hinz, Walther
1973   *Neue Wege im Altpersischen*. Göttinger Orientforschungen. Wiesbaden: Harrassowitz.

Hoffner, Harry A., Jr.
1990   *Hittite Myths*. SBLWAW 2. Atlanta: Scholars Press.

Hoftijzer, Jacob, and K. Jongeling
1995   *Dictionary of the North-West Semitic Inscriptions*. Handbuch der Orientalistik. Erste Abteilung, Der Nahe und Mittlere Osten 21/1–2. Leiden: Brill.

Holladay, John S.
1976   "Of Sherds and Strata: Contributions toward an Understanding of the Archaeology of the Divided Monarchy." Pages 253–93 in *Magnalia Dei: The Mighty Acts of God*. Edited by Frank Moore Cross, Werner Lemke, and Patrick D. Miller. Garden City, N.Y.: Doubleday.

Jastrow, Marcus
1903   *A Dictionary of the Targumim, the Talmud Babli and Yerushalmi, and the Midrashic Literature*. New York: Jastrow.

Kaufman, Stephen A.
1974   *Akkadian Influences on Aramaic*. Oriental Institute Assyriological Studies 19. Chicago: University of Chicago Press.

Kaufman, Stephen A., Joseph A. Fitzmyer, and Michael Sokoloff, eds.
2001   "CAL Bibliographic Resources." *The Comprehensive Aramaic Lexicon*. http://cal1.cn.huc.edu/bibliography/index.html (30 June 2002).

Kent, R. G.
1953   *Old Persian: Grammar, Texts, Lexicon*. American Oriental Series 33. New Haven: American Oriental Society.

Kornfeld, Walter
1978   *Onomastica aramaica aus Ägypten*. Österreichische Akademie der Wissenschaften, Philosophisch-historiche Klasse: Sitzungsberichte 333. Vienna: Österreichische Akademie der Wissenschaften.

Kraeling, Emil G.

    1953   *The Brooklyn Museum Aramaic Papyri*. New Haven: Yale University Press.

Lemaire, André

    1977   *Les ostraca*. Vol. 1 of *Inscriptions hébraïques*. Littératures anciennes du proche-orient 9. Paris: Cerf.

    1984   "Who or What Was Yahweh's Asherah?" *BAR* 10.6:42–51.

Lemaire, André, and Jean-Marie Durand

    1984   *Les inscriptions araméennes de Sfiré et l'Assyrie de Shamshi-Ilu*. École pratique des hautes études; IVe Section, Sciences historiques et philologiques. II Hautes études orientales, no. 20. Geneva and Paris: Droz.

Levine, Baruch A.

    1964   "Notes on an Aramaic Dream Text from Egypt." *JAOS* 84:18–22.

    1969   "Notes on a Hebrew Ostracon from Arad." *IEJ* 19:49–51.

Lidzbarski, Mark

    1903–7   *Ephemeris für semitische Epigraphik 2*. Giessen: Töpelmann.

    1909–15 *Ephemeris für semitische Epigraphik 3*. Giessen: Töpelmann.

    1921   *Altaramäische Urkunden aus Assur*. Ausgrabungen der Deutschen Orient-Gesellschaft in Assur. E and V Altaramäische Urkunden. Leipzig: Hinrichs.

Lim, Timothy

    2000   "Kittim." Pages 469–71 in vol. 1 of *Encyclopedia of the Dead Sea Scrolls*. Edited by Lawrence H. Schiffman and James C. VanderKam. Oxford: Oxford University Press.

Lindenberger, James M.

    1984   *The Aramaic Proverbs of Ahiqar*. Baltimore: Johns Hopkins University Press.

    2001   "What Ever Happened to Vidranga? A Jewish Liturgy of Cursing from Elephantine." Pages 134–57 in *The World of the Aramaeans III: Studies in Honour of Paul Eugène Dion*. Edited by P. M. Michèle Daviau, John W. Wevers, and Michael Weigl. Sheffield: Sheffield Academic Press.

Lozachmeur, Hélène

    1971   "Un ostracon araméen inédit d'Éléphantine (Collection Clermont-Ganneau No 228)." *Semitica* 21:81–93.

    1990   "Un ostracon araméen d'Éléphantine (Collection Clermont-Ganneau no 125?)." *Semitica* 39:29–36.

Lyle, Evelyn

    1966   *The Search for the Royal Road*. London: Vision.

Malamat, Abraham

    1968   "The Last Kings of Judah and the Fall of Jerusalem." *IEJ* 18:137–56.

1975   "The Twilight of Judah: In the Egyptian-Babylonian Mael-
            strom." Pages 123–45 in *Congress Volume: Edinburgh 1974*.
            Supplements to Vetus Testamentum 28. Leiden: Brill.

Mazar, A.
1981   "The Excavations at Khirbet Abu et-Twein and the System of
            Iron Age Fortresses in Judah" [Hebrew]. *Eretz Israel* 15:229–49
            [Eng. summary, pp. 83*–84*].

McCarter, P. Kyle
1999   "The Divided Monarchy: The Kingdoms of Judah and
            Israel." Pages 129–99 in *Ancient Israel: From Abraham to
            the Roman Destruction of the Temple*. Edited by Hershel
            Shanks. Washington, D.C.: Prentice Hall/Biblical Archaeol-
            ogy Society.

McLaughlin, John L.
2001   *The Marzeah in the Prophetic Literature: References and
            Allusions in Light of the Extra-Biblical Evidence*. Leiden:
            Brill.

Meshel, Ze'ev
1978   *Kuntillet 'Ajrud: A Religious Centre from the Time of the
            Judean Monarchy on the Border of Sinai*. Israel Museum Cat-
            alog 175. Jerusalem: Israel Museum.

Meshel, Ze'ev, and Carol Meyers
1976   "The Name of God in the Wilderness of Zin." *BA* 39:6–10.

Milik, J. T.
1961   "Textes hébreux et araméens." Pages 67–205 in *Les grottes de
            Murabba'ât*. DJD 2. Oxford: Clarendon.
1967   "Les papyrus araméens d'Hermopolis et les cultes syro-
            phéniciens en Égypte perse." *Biblica* 48:546–628.

Miller, Patrick D.
1971   "The Mrzh Text." Pages 37–54 in *The Claremont Ras Shamra
            Tablets*. Edited by Loren R. Fisher. Analecta orientalia 48.
            Rome: Pontificium institutum biblicum.
2000   *The Religion of Ancient Israel*. Library of Ancient Israel.
            Louisville: Westminster John Knox; London: SPCK.

Moorey, P. R. S.
1988   "The Persian Empire." Pages 1–94 in *Persia, Greece and the
            Western Mediterranean, c. 525–479 B.C.* [plates]. Edited by
            John Boardman. Supplement to vol. 4 of *The Cambridge
            Ancient History*. Cambridge: Cambridge University Press.

Muraoka, Takamitsu, and Bezalel Porten
1998   *A Grammar of Egyptian Aramaic*. Handbuch der Oriental-
            istik. Erste Abteilung: Der nahe und mittlere Osten 32.
            Leiden: Brill.

Naveh, Joseph
  1960   "A Hebrew Letter from the Seventh Century." *IEJ* 10:129–39.
  1962   "The Excavation at Mesad Hashavyahu: Preliminary Report."
            IEJ 12:89–113.
  1970   *The Development of the Aramaic Script*. Jerusalem: Israel
            Academy of Sciences and Humanities.
  1979   "Graffiti and Dedications." *BASOR* 235:27–30.
Naveh, Joseph, and Saul Shaked
  1971   "A Recently Published Aramaic Papyrus." *JAOS* 91:379–82.
Oded, Bustenay
  1977   "Judah and the Exile." Pages 435–88 in *Israelite and Judean
            History*. Edited by John H. Hayes and J. Maxwell Miller.
            Philadelphia: Westminster.
  1979   *Mass Deportations and Deportees in the Neo-Assyrian Empire*.
            Wiesbaden: Reichert.
Olmstead, A. T.
  1948   *History of the Persian Empire*. Chicago: University of Chicago
            Press.
Olyan, Saul
  1988   *Asherah and the Cult of Yahweh in Israel*. Atlanta: Scholars
            Press.
Oppenheim, A. Leo
  1977   *Ancient Mesopotamia: Portrait of a Dead Civilization*. Revised
            by Erica Reiner. Chicago: University of Chicago Press.
  1985   "The Babylonian Evidence of Achaemenian Rule in Meso-
            potamia." Pages 529–87 in *The Median and Achaemenian
            Periods*. Edited by Ilya Gershevitch. Vol. 2 of *The Cambridge
            History of Iran*. Cambridge: Cambridge University Press.
Pardee, Dennis
  1978a   "The Judicial Plea from Meṣad Ḥashavyahu (Yavneh-Yam): A
            New Philological Study." *Maarav* 1:33–66.
  1978b   "Letters from Tel Arad." *Ugarit-Forschungen* 10:289–336.
  1982   *Handbook of Ancient Hebrew Letters*. With S. David Sperling,
            J. David Whitehead, and Paul-Eugène Dion. Society of Bibli-
            cal Literature Sources for Biblical Study 15. Chico, Calif.:
            Scholars Press.
  2002   "Hebrew Letters." Pages 77–86 in *Archival Documents from
            the Biblical World*. Vol. 3 of *The Context of Scripture*. Edited
            by William W. Hallo and K. Lawson Younger Jr. Leiden:
            Brill.
Porada, Edith
  1985   "Classic Achaemenian Architecture and Sculpture." Pages
            793–827 in *The Median and Achaemenian Periods*. Edited by

Ilya Gershevitch. Vol. 2 of *The Cambridge History of Iran.* Cambridge: Cambridge University Press.

Porten, Bezalel

1968 *Archives from Elephantine: The Life of an Ancient Jewish Military Colony.* Berkeley and Los Angeles: University of California Press.

1979 "Aramaic Papyri and Parchments: A New Look." *BA* 42:74–104.

1980 "Aramaic Letters: A Study in Papyrological Reconstruction. *Journal of the American Research Center in Egypt* 17:39–75.

1981 "The Identity of King Adon." *BA* 44:36–52.

1984 "The Diaspora: D. The Jews in Egypt." Pages 372–400 in *Introduction; The Persian Period.* Edited by W. D. Davies and Louis Finkelstein. Vol. 1 of *The Cambridge History of Judaism.* Cambridge: Cambridge University Press.

1997 "Review of James M. Lindenberger, *Ancient Aramaic and Hebrew Letters* (Scholars Press: 1994)." *JAOS* 117:370–71.

Porten, Bezalel, J. Joel Farber, et al.

1996 *The Elephantine Papyri in English: Three Millennia of Cross-Cultural Continuity and Change.* Documenta et monumenta orientis antiqui: Studies in Near Eastern Archaeology and Civilisation 22. Leiden: Brill.

Porten, Bezalel, and Jonas C. Greenfield

1974 *Jews of Elephantine and Arameans of Syene: Aramaic Texts with Translations.* Jerusalem: Academon.

Porten, Bezalel, and Ada Yardeni

1986 *Letters.* Vol. 1 of *Textbook of Aramaic Documents from Ancient Egypt.* The Hebrew University Department of the History of the Jewish People, Texts and Studies for Students. Winona Lake, Ind.: Eisenbrauns.

1989 *Contracts.* Vol. 2 of *Textbook of Aramaic Documents from Ancient Egypt.* The Hebrew University Department of the History of the Jewish People, Texts and Studies for Students. Winona Lake, Ind.: Eisenbrauns.

1991 "Three Unpublished Aramaic Ostraca." *Maarav* 7:207–29.

1999 *Ostraca and Assorted Inscriptions.* Vol. 4 of *Textbook of Aramaic Documents from Ancient Egypt.* The Hebrew University Department of the History of the Jewish People, Texts and Studies for Students. Winona Lake, Ind.: Eisenbrauns.

Price, M. Jessop

1988 "Coinage." Pages 237–48 in *Persia, Greece and the Western Mediterranean, c. 525–479 B.C.* [plates]. Edited by John

Boardman. Vol. 4 of *The Cambridge Ancient History.* Cambridge: Cambridge University Press.

Pritchard, James B., ed.
1969   *Ancient Near Eastern Texts Relating to the Old Testament.* 3d ed. Princeton: Princeton University Press.

Renz, Johannes
1995   *Die althebräischen Inschriften.* Part 1: *Text und Kommentar;* Part 2: *Zusammenfassende Erörterungen, Paläographie und Glossar.* Handbuch der althebräischen Epigraphik I–II/1. Darmstadt: Wissenschaftliche Buchgesellschaft.
1997   *Schrift und Schreibertradition: Eine paläographische Studie zum kulturgeschichtlichen Verhältnis von israelitischem Nordreich und Südreick.* Abhandlungen des deutschen Palästina-Vereins 23. Wiesbaden: Harrassowitz.

Renz, Johannes, and Wolfgang Röllig
1995   *Texte und Tafeln.* Vol. 3 of *Handbuch der althebräischen Epigraphik.* Darmstadt: Wissenschaftliche Buchgesellschaft.

Ridgway, David
1988   "Italy." Pages 202–36 in *Persia, Greece and the Western Mediterranean, c. 525–479 B.C.* [plates]. Edited by John Boardman. Vol. 4 of *The Cambridge Ancient History.* Cambridge: Cambridge University Press.

Rollston, Chris A.
1998   "Are They Genuine? Laboratory Analysis of the Moussaïeff Ostraca Using the Scanning Electron Microscope (SEM) with an Energy Dispersive X-Ray Microanalyzer (EDS)." *Near Eastern Archaeology* 61:8–9.

Rosenthal, Franz
1961   *A Grammar of Biblical Aramaic.* Porta linguarum orientalium NS 5. Wiesbaden: Harrassowitz.

Rosenthal, Franz, ed.
1967   *An Aramaic Handbook.* Porta linguarum orientalium NS 10. Wiesbaden: Harrassowitz.

Sachau, Edouard
1911   *Aramäische Papyrus und Ostraka aus einer jüdischen Militär-kolonie zu Elephantine.* Leipzig: Hinrichs.

Saggs, H. W. F.
1984   *The Might That Was Assyria.* London: Sidgwick & Jackson.

Sayce, A. H.
1909   "An Aramaic Ostracon from Elephantine, Part 1." *Proceedings of the Society of Biblical Archaeology* 31:154–55.
1911   "An Aramaic Ostracon from Elephantine, Part 2." *Proceedings of the Society of Biblical Archaeology* 33:183–84.

Sayce, A. H., and A. E. Cowley
1906   *Aramaic Papyri Discovered at Assuan.* London: A. Moring.
Schwiderski, Dirk
2000   *Handbuch des nordsemitischen Briefformulars.* BZAW 295. Berlin: de Gruyter.
Segal, J. B.
1983   *Aramaic Texts from North Saqqâra.* Excavations at North Saqqâra 4. Documentary Series. London: Egypt Exploration Society.
Sérandour, Arnaud
1998   "King, Priest, and Temple." *Near Eastern Archaeology* 61:6.
Shanks, Hershel
1997   "Three Shekels for the Lord." *BAR* 23.6:28–32.
Smelik, Klaas A. D.
1991   *Writings from Ancient Israel: A Handbook of Historical and Religious Documents.* Louisville: Westminster John Knox.
Smith, Morton
1971   *Palestinian Parties and Politics That Shaped the Old Testament.* New York: Columbia University Press.
1984   "Jewish Religious Life in the Persian Period." Pages 219–78 in *Introduction; The Persian Period.* Edited by W. D. Davies and Louis Finkelstein. Vol. 1 of *The Cambridge History of Judaism.* Cambridge: Cambridge University Press.
Soden, Wolfram von
1965–81 *Akkadisches Handwörterbuch.* 3 vols. Wiesbaden: Harrassowitz.
Sokoloff, Michael
1990   *A Dictionary of Jewish Palestinian Aramaic.* Ramat Gan: Bar Ilan University Press.
Stark, Jürgen Kurt
1971   *Personal Names in Palmyrene Inscriptions.* Oxford: Clarendon.
Torczyner [Tur-Sinai], Harry
1938   *The Lachish Letters.* Lachish 1. London: Oxford University Press.
Vattioni, F.
1970   "Epigraphia aramaica." *Augustinianum* 10:493–532.
Vincent, Albert
1937   *La religion des judéo-araméens d'Éléphantine.* Paris: Paul Geuthner.
Waltke, Bruce K., and Michael Patrick O'Connor
1990   *An Introduction to Biblical Hebrew Syntax.* Winona Lake,

Ind.: Eisenbrauns.

Wente, Edward

1990 *Letters from Ancient Egypt.* SBLWAW 1. Atlanta: Scholars Press.

Whitehead, J. David

1974 "Early Aramaic Epistolography: The Arsames Correspondence." Ph.D. dissertation. University of Chicago.

1978 "Some Distinctive Features of the Language of the Aramaic Arsames Correspondence." *JNES* 37:119–40.

Wilson, R. J. A.

1988 "The Western Greeks." Pages 179–201 in *Persia, Greece and the Western Mediterranean, c. 525–479 B.C.* [plates]. Edited by John Boardman. Vol. 4 of *The Cambridge Ancient History.* Cambridge: Cambridge University Press.

Wiseman, D. J.

1956 *Chronicles of Chaldean Kings, 626–556, in the British Museum.* London: British Museum.

1958 *The Vassal-Treaties of Esarhaddon.* London: British School of Archaeology in Iraq.

Yadin, Yigael

1984 "The Lachish Letters—Originals or Copies and Drafts?" Pages 179–86 in *Recent Archaeology in the Land of Israel.* Edited by Hershel Shanks and Benjamin Mazar. Washington, D.C.: Biblical Archaeology Society.

Yassine, Khair, and Javier Teixidor

1986 "Ammonite and Aramaic Inscriptions from Tell El-Mazār in Jordan." *BASOR* 264:45–50.

Yeivin, S.

1962 "The Judicial Petition from Mezad Hashavyahu." *Bibliotheca orientalis* 19:3–10.

Glossary

ardab. A measure of capacity used in Egypt, approximately thirty liters (27 dry quarts). The size of a farm can be indicated by giving the number of *ardabs* of seed sown in it.

bath. A liquid measure roughly equivalent to twenty-two liters (5.5 liquid gallons), or about twice that amount, according to some.

Baal-Saphon (Baal Zephon). An ancient Canaanite high god, worshiped in Syria from the mid-second millennium. He was also known among the Semites in northern Egypt, where a town was named for him (Exod 14:2, 9).

Banit. Epithet of a divinity worshiped at Syene. Banit has been uncertainly identified with the Babylonian goddess Zarpanitu, consort of Marduk and mother of Nabu.

Beel-Shemayn (Baal Shamayim). "The Lord of Heaven," high god widely venerated among the Aramean and Canaanite peoples of Syria and northern Mesopotamia. Some reckoned him as chief of the pantheon.

Bes. A minor Egyptian god, often associated with children and childbirth. Bes is depicted as a grotesque dwarf with bow legs, a jug head, and a tail.

Bethel. Epithet of a West Semitic divinity worshiped in Syria-Palestine; literally "the house of God" or "the house of the god El." Bethel had a temple at Syene, and many Aramean personal names from Egypt are compounded with the name.

cubit. A unit of linear measure used in Egypt, Mesopotamia, and Israel. This measure was based on the distance from the elbow to the tip of the middle finger; there was no universal standard length. Measuring sticks found in Egypt indicate a long cubit (sometimes called "royal") of about 52.5 centimeters (20.6 inches) and a shorter cubit of approximately 45 centimeters (18 inches). There were long and short cubits also in Israel.

homer. A large measure of dry capacity used particularly for grain. Originally a donkey-load, the *homer* may never have been precisely defined, although most modern scholars estimate it between 134 and 209 liters (3.8 and 5 bushels).

Ishtar. Mesopotamian goddess of fertility and war. Her chief shrine was in Arbela.

karsh. The official standard of weight for silver in the Persian Empire, the *karsh* weighed slightly less than ten Egyptian shekels. An extra *zuz* (half-shekel) was often added to the *karsh* to bring it up to ten-shekel weight, hence the conversion formula "one *zuz* to the ten," in economic documents of the period (Porten 1968: 66–67, 305–7).

Khnum. The Egyptian ram god, guardian of the First Cataract of the Nile. His main temple was on the island of Elephantine, not far from the Jewish temple of YHW.

letech. A unit of dry measure, probably equal to one-half *homer*.

Marheshwan. The eighth month of the Babylonian-Jewish calendar, equivalent to October–November in the Julian calendar.

marzeah. Apparently a voluntary society that celebrated festal banquets in honor of the dead. There is scattered evidence for such associations in inscriptions from different parts of the Near East from the fourteenth century B.C.E. down to the third century C.E., including the Hebrew Bible (Amos 6:7; Jer 16:5) and in rabbinic sources (*Sipre Num.* 131; *Midr. Lev. Rab.* 5:3; *b. Mo'ed Qat.* 28b; *b. Ketub.* 8b, 69ab; *y. Ber.* 2:6a, top). See Porten 1968: 179–86; Miller 1971; and McLaughlin 2001.

Mehir. The sixth month in the Egyptian calendar, corresponding to Siwan, third month in the Babylonian-Jewish calendar (May–June).

mina. A medium unit of weight, equal to sixty shekels.

Nisan. First month in the Babylonian-Jewish calendar (March–April).

Nabu. Babylonian god, son of Marduk and Zarpanitu. Nabu was especially prominent in the late Neo-Babylonian period.

Ptah. Egyptian creator god whose primary place of worship was Memphis.

qab. A measure of capacity equivalent to slightly over one liter (about one dry quart).

Quas (Qos). The national divinity of ancient Edom.

Queen of Heaven. A high goddess who had a temple in Syene. The epithet refers to the ancient Canaanite goddess of love and warfare known variously as Anath, Asherah, and Astarte, or possibly her Babylonian counterpart, Ishtar. According to Jer 7:18; 44:17–19, 25, the Queen of Heaven was venerated by Judean refugees fleeing to Upper Egypt in Jeremiah's time.

shekel. A unit of weight calculated at Elephantine as 8.76 grams (.31 ounce). Some shekel weights from monarchic Israel weigh around 11.4

grams, and there was also a "heavy" shekel weighing nearly twice as much as the Elephantine shekel.

talent. A large unit of weight, equal to 360 shekels.

Tammuz. Fourth month in the Babylonian-Jewish calendar, named for the dying and rising vegetation god (June–July).

Tebeth. Tenth month in the Babylonian-Jewish calendar (December–January).

YHH, YHW, YHWH. Variant forms of the consonants forming the name of the God of Israel. The first two forms appear in Aramaic texts from Egypt; the third is the usual Hebrew form.

zuz. A half-shekel.

Indexes

1. Deities

Gender cannot always be determined, but names clearly identified as feminine are so indicated.

2. Personal Names

Language and regional abbreviations: Akk = Akkadian, Amm = Ammonite, Anat = Anatolian, Arab = Arabic, Can = Canaanite, Ed = Edomite, Eg = Egyptian, Gk = Greek, Pers = Persian, Phoen = Phoenician. Names with no indication are Hebrew, Aramaic, or generic Northwest Semitic (or are names generally known from ancient history). It is not always possible to distinguish between Akkadian and West Semitic names and frequently impossible to distinguish between Aramaic, Hebrew, and Canaanite. Bib. indicates conventional spelling in English versions of the Bible. Egyptian and Persian names commonly cited in Greek form are indicated as follows: Achaemenes (Pers > Gk).

3. Places

4. Subjects

5. Biblical, Qumran, Rabbinic, and Early Christian Literature